What Do Parents' Narratives Reveal About Their Experience with Their Child's IEP?

Carletta L. Bryant Ph.D

authorHOUSE®

AuthorHouse™
1663 Liberty Drive
Bloomington, IN 47403
www.authorhouse.com
Phone: 1 (800) 839-8640

Published by AuthorHouse 12/30/2016

ISBN: 978-1-5246-0566-7 (sc)
ISBN: 978-1-5246-0564-3 (hc)
ISBN: 978-1-5246-0565-0 (e)

Library of Congress Control Number: 2016906816

Print information available on the last page.

This book is printed on acid-free paper.

Table of Contents

PREFACE

The inception of this work comes from the most precious and valuable happenings of my life…the birth and life interactions with my son Mason Charles Bryant. I would have never imagined this being my life i.e. being the mother of a child who lives with cognitive disabilities and also medically fragile. To that end, as Mason's mother, I could never have dreamed of acquiring the joy, pain and knowledge that transcends to an enormous appetite to learn and educate. Mason's existence has challenged me and taken me to spaces I never thought I would go. Inescapably, I am a better human being, mother, advocate, educator, agent of transformation, professional, and leader because of him.

This book demonstrates how a researcher's transparent interestedness and multiple identities as a mother of a child who is identified under the federal disability category "multiple disabilities" with an IEP and an authority on education conveys more trustworthiness than the illusion of disinterestedness that has traditionally been practiced in qualitative inquiry. These multiple identities have been simultaneously a curse and a blessing. Having these multiple lenses has made me privy to various perspectives and accept the responsibility to be transparent. Candidly speaking it has been my mother identity that has forced my other identities to confront, challenge and encourage each other.

You will often hear the phrase "who lives with special needs" in this book. As odd as this may sound to some, it makes a lot of sense to those of us who care for a child who lives with special needs; as we know as caregivers that our children are not defined by their disability. Our children supersede their conditions. In other words, Mason is not a special needs child. Mason champions his cognitive and medical conditions; therefore "he lives with these special needs".

In chapter 4: Results, I share parents' experiences with their child's individualized educational program (IEP) discerned through their own narratives. I illustrate some of their stories metaphorically through categorized classical or popular stories, films, or aphorisms in hopes that the reader can understand the parents' narratives through a mutual place of knowing. A short summary is given of each classical or popular story, film, or aphorism as they were produced from the salient themes drawn from the parents' narratives. Next, an analogy of the parents' narratives is written to appreciate the juxtaposition to the classical or popular story, film, or aphorism. Finally, portions of the parents' actual narratives are analyzed, interpreted, and shared. The reader will find that several of the themes overlap as some excerpts could have been placed in two or three categories. Presented in this chapter are very different stories but similar experiences.

The intent of this book is to affirm parents and families of children who live with special needs but also allow professionals to hear and understand the perspective of these parents and families and improve the IEP process. Parents' narratives can potentially provide important information about how they and their children experience the IEP process. These parents' reflective accounts of their children while navigating a special academic system command the attention of all stakeholders.

This book will also create awareness and challenge assumptions among those stakeholders involved in the development of an IEP. It is with intent that this work will sensitize special education professionals about parents' experiences in the IEP process. When school officials listen and understand the experiences of parents involving their children, a collaborative effort from a collective body of knowledge can be the basis for decisions regarding the individualized education plan in the best interest of that child.

"It is my mission to **ILLUMINATE** the darkness of a limited mindset; **EXPOSE** the practices of those who marginalize those who are *"othered"*; **EMPOWER** those who desire knowledge to become agents of change. I believe life is sacred and all life deserves dignity. I envision a society that embraces differences among individuals and not only recognize when individuals are *"othered"* but have the advocating spirit to speak against it".

~Dr. Carletta L. Bryant

SPECIAL DEDICATION

This book is dedicated to my colleague and childhood friend Dr. Monica Marks who altruistically inspired me to publish my book. Dr. Marks has graced those around her with a wealth of humanity, knowledge and most importantly a giving spirit filled with love. Monica you and your advocating spirit will be missed as I know you are a special angel in heaven watching over us.

In the inspirational words of Eunice Kennedy Shriver *"Let me win. If I cannot win, let me be brave in my attempt."*

Dr. Marks you championed your fight with cancer because you exemplified courage, dignity and strength. Who *led* a staff, *inspired* students, *completed* a Ph.D Program and *published* a book? Dr. Monica Marks did…THAT'S WHO!

In Remembrance
Of
Monica L. Marks Ph.D. 1970-2016

DEDICATION

First and foremost I must give all praise and honor to God and my Lord Jesus Christ for being the head of my life. There were one set of footprints in my PhD journey. HE carried me all the way. To my mother and father, Charles and Mattie Davidson—my childhood was rich with love and support by two great parents who instilled the value of education in their children. Daddy, I know you are looking down on me smiling with proudness. To my husband, Mark, you supported my endeavor and made just as many sacrifices as I. My sisters Mildred (Cookie) and Tawnyell you are my right and left lung...I could not breathe without you both. My brother and brothers-in-law, David, Datalion and Tony your encouragement and selfless acts are appreciated. My nephew, Chas, you inspired me in ways you would never know. To my cousin-sister Donna, thank you for your love and support and always checking in on my progress. To our home health care group, "Team Mason" I could not have completed this degree without your tender-loving-care (TLC) and nursing skills that allowed me not only to have a piece of mind while away from my son but for me to rest at night to only do it all over again the next day. Special thanks to Mack and Sylvia Bottorf for your support and unwavering love for Mason. You guys are an extension of our family and like grandparents to Mason. Thank you to my Aunts Geraldine, Mondine, Uncle Chris and my Sands of Delta Sigma Theta Sorority. Thanks to all my family and friends

ACKNOWLEDGEMENTS

There are no words of accolades that could adequately express my gratitude to the professors in Educational Leadership PhD Program at Miami University for my bourgeoning scholarship. Many thanks to my dissertation committee for your outstanding support Dr. Denise Baszile, Dr. Sally Lloyd, Dr. Paula Saine and Dr. Richard Quantz. Special thanks to my Dissertation Director Dr. Baszile you have always encouraged me to be true to my subjectivity and creativity in all my work throughout this program. Special thanks to my Dissertation Co-Director Dr. Quantz you were my ROCK through my dissertation process. Where others have been intimidated by your presence and intelligence I was drawn to it. I knew you would hold me to my scholarship and I am most appreciative for that.challenged me and taken me to spaces I never thought I would go. Inescapably, I am a better human being, mother, advocate, educator, agent of transformation, professional, and leader because of him.

CHAPTER 1: INTRODUCTION TO STUDY

To listen and describe how parents feel about their child's IEP through their experiences provides a missing voice in our understanding of that process. My interpretive study was guided by two basic assumptions: 1. knowledge is socially constructed, and 2. researchers should attempt to comprehend the lived phenomenon from the point of view of those who lived it. What insight can we gain from the stories of these parents' experiences behind and beyond the doors of an IEP meeting? How does this knowledge gained inform parents' involvement? Hearing a parent's perspective of their child's IEP produces a gateway to the experience. Excluding such information may be the elucidation that increases knowledge to eradicate maladaptive practices and affirm and/or develop the positive behaviors needed to afford parents a productive experience in the IEP process (Garriott, P. P., Wandry, D., & Snyder, L, 2000).

Statement of the Problem

There is an absence of parents' voices in research on the IEP. Thus, this study is intended not only to listen and provide a missing voice in our understanding of the individualized education program (IEP) through the experiences offered in the narratives of ten parents who have children on IEPs, but also to examine what those experiences tell us about how issues of power inform the process.

Today, parents have the right to play an essential role in their child's special education process. The Individuals with Disabilities Education Act (IDEA) amendments of 1997 unequivocally state that parents are to be included as members of the IEP. "Each public agency must take steps to ensure that one or both of the parents of a child with a disability are present at each IEP Team meeting or are afforded the opportunity to participate" (Individuals with Disabilities Education Act, 1997 Sec. 300.322 Parent participation). The traditional roles of parents as "passive participants" in their child's education is being challenged more, thus viewing parents as having valuable knowledge concerning their child's special educational process. This is especially true for the process of IEPs. This would resemble more family-centered practices versus child-centered practices (Turnbull &

Turnbull, 1997).

Purpose of the Study

The purpose of this study was to provide a parent perspective

about the IEP in order to improve this process for parents. Parents'

narratives can potentially provide important information about how

they and their children experience IEP process. This will also create

awareness and challenge assumptions among those stakeholders

involved in the development of an IEP. This study should inform and

sensitize special education professionals about parents' experiences in

the IEP process (Pruitt, Wandry, & Hollums, 1998). In other words,

when school officials listen and understand the experiences of parents

involving their children, a collaborative effort from a collective body

of knowledge can be the basis for decisions regarding the

individualized education plan in the best interest of that child. Thus, to

bridge experiences is to build on perspectives (Garriott, P. P., Wandry,

D., & Snyder, L., 2000). The reflective account of parents who raise a

child who lives with disabilities while navigating a special academic

3

system commands the attention of all stakeholders. Valle (2011) echoes that parents', particularly mothers', narratives inform us of the effects of what is not working in educational practices in their lives.

Question for the Study

The research question for this study is "What do parents' narratives reveal about their experience with their child's IEP?" In answering this question, several sub-questions were also pursued including but not limited to: What do parents' narratives reveal about how power is negotiated? To what extent do parents' narratives suggest that they felt as if their voices were heard in the process? What did parents' narratives reveal about metamessages? How did parents' narratives describe their comprehension of the dialogue? To what extent do these narratives suggest that parents felt included or excluded? To what degree do parents' narratives illustrate a spirit of encouragement in the longevity of the process? And, to what extent do these narratives reveal an experience that parents felt actually worked in the best interest of their child?

Stories from Multiple Identities

Everyone has a story or stories whether they know it or not. Throughout cultures, stories in many forms have been around as long as human life has existed. Jean Clandinin and Michael Connelly (2000) explain that people live their stories because stories are their experiences: "People live stories, and in the telling of these stories, reaffirm them, modify them, and create new ones. Stories lived and told educate the self and others, including the young and those such as researchers who are new to their communities" (p. xxvi). Perhaps this is why people can make meaning of things when conveyed in a story (Polkinghorne, 1988).

The birth of this research comes from my personal story as a mother who so happens to be an authority on education and has a child who lives with special needs and is also medically fragile. These multiple identities have been simultaneously a curse and a blessing. Having these multiple lenses has made me privy to various perspectives and the responsibility I have to be transparent and to embrace them. Honestly, it has been my mother identity that has forced my other identities to confront each other. As Mason's mother, I could never have dreamed of acquiring the joy, pain and knowledge that would transcend and manifest in an enormous appetite to learn and educate. Mason's existence has challenged me and taken me to spaces I never thought I would go. Inescapably, I am a better human being, mother, advocate, educator, agent of transformation, professional, and leader because of him.

The following are my short- story versions of these multiple identities, i.e educator, researcher, and mother that are attached to my being.

Educator

I can remember as a fresh -young teacher right out of school sitting in my first IEP meeting. Sadly, I didn't know what an IEP was until I was asked to participate as the student's current teacher. I can't recall anyone ever explaining to me the significance of this document. Oh, I do remember as a regular education pre-service teacher reading a chapter on special education in one of my required courses. I distinctly remember coming to the realization, while in the meeting, that this was something I was supposed to be responsible for and more importantly following through on. Perhaps it was not brought to my attention because I was a regular education teacher who happened to have a student on an IEP. As important as this IEP appeared to be, why wasn't I made aware of this? How was this overlooked? Where was the communication breakdown? I received the notice to participate in the IEP meeting but I did not get the description of my role in this document. What does this say about the value or lack of for this document? What does this say about the significance of each stakeholder, especially the student? My future involvement with IEP meetings as a teacher became worse. As I began to come to the realization about the purpose of this document and all the politics that came along with it, the more I felt like a hypocrite. "The parents, these poor parents," I would say to myself as I starred in their faces, "have no clue about the process because honestly we have no clue." We sit here speaking in our educational jargon, with our advanced degrees, professional opinions, and our nerve. Our nerve to leave this table and carry on with business as usual until we come back again to meet. I do not recall having the on-going conversations or interactions with the special education teacher that, as I now understand, was critical to ensure the best education for the student on the IEP. Again, I realized that I was just the regular education teacher but I signed my name on this document that signified I was a key player on the team. Why didn't I speak out? Did I think I was too much of a novice and wouldn't be heard? Perhaps, I would have been marginalized as not being a team player for speaking out. I used to feel badly for those parents who would look like deer in the headlights or plainly sad and powerless while we shared not very good information about their children. I never recalled parents being active participants in these meetings; they just sat motionless and received the information. I am not sure if they even realized that they had the right to be more vocal. I am not confident that we, as educators, even knew they could have a voice in the matter.

"Good teachers need to have both dominant and cooperative understandings of their students, and the same qualities for working with families" (Wubbels, Levy, & Brekelmans, 1997 p.37). As an educator, I also served in the position as a Parent Resource Teacher which involved being a parent advocate and school ambassador. This position was designed to mend and secure the connectedness of family, community, and school. This position sounds positive for the district's initiative for family involvement. Unfortunately, in my experience, sustaining a safe space to hear the voices of families, and especially those who may have felt "othered," did not exist.

"There is no child whose intellectual, social, and emotional development is without struggle or injury" (Lawrence-Lightfoot, 2003 p. 92). For that reason alone, our job as strategic leaders is never complete because there should always be a space for inquiry. I am still haunted by a young boy's cry not to be placed in the special education class that he was previously assigned to prior to enrolling in our district. As the Parent Resource Teacher, it was my job to escort this terrified child to his nightmare. What a way to be welcomed into a new school district. This child's cry was not of being introduced to his "typical" new classroom of peers and teacher, but unequivocally being placed into a "special education class". He was suspicious when he entered the classroom occupied by others who more than likely carried an equal stigma of being different. What prior events occurred that confirmed his instincts about being led to this "special class" I would never know. It could have been the décor of the classroom, the demeanor or expressions on the faces of the other students, the unfriendly face of his new teacher, my unprepared babbling of sugarcoating his destination, or the penetrating stares and volumes of silence upon our entrance. Most importantly, what was this child's previous classroom experience that made him so full of anxiety to enter into this classroom? These are questions of a strategic educator. I did not know the answers to any of these questions. Unfortunately, this classroom teacher's welcome was flat and unfriendly—just down right "bitchy". I felt intimidated and I was a colleague! I could only imagine how this student felt. His reality could never be experienced by someone who has never been ostracized and labeled. This scenario was placed into perspective for me after I envisioned the child praying the night before that his paper trail of labels would become lost and this was his chance to attend school without stigmas, judgments, deviant adornments, and with just a "normal" label. How disappointing and disheartening the reality must have been for him as I walked him down the "hall of shame". What conversations did his family have with him the night before or morning before coming to this new school? More importantly, where was his family? Would I get a call from his family asking how the child got along for his first day? Although I was disturbed by this event, I went on with my day as usual—I forgot about this child. I dropped the ball! It was not my intention but I became caught up in the tasks of the day. How many of us as educators get caught up in those daily tasks that we forget "the real task"—which is to ensure that all students and families and especially the marginalized feel comfortable and welcomed into our schools and districts.

Mother

Where do I began? The illustrious Mrs. Edna Massionilla personally gave me permission to use the following poem that illustrates the beautiful making of my amazing son Mason.

Once Upon A Time

A meeting was held, quite far from earth
"It's time again for another birth"
Said the Angels to the Lord above,
"This special child will need much love"

His progress may seem very slow,
Accomplishments he may not show
And he'll require extra care
From all the people he meets down there.

He may not run or laugh or play
His thoughts may seem quite far away
In many ways he won't adapt,
And he'll be labeled as handicapped.

So let's be careful where this little one is sent
we want his life to be content
Please, Lord, find the right parents who
will do this special job for you.

They will not realize right away
the leading role they're asked to play
but with him sent from above
Comes stronger faith and richer love.

*And soon they will know the privilege given
in caring for this gift from Heaven.
Their precious charge, so meek and mild
is heaven's very special child.*

Author: Edna Massionilla, December 1981

Who am I to have been given the blessing and yet the curse of being the mother of a child who lives with special needs, i.e., intellectually delayed and medically fragile? I would have never chosen this life. I applaud those who willingly adopt this lifestyle without having family ties. However, if God offered me a perfectly healthy son in exchange for my son I would unequivocally reply **"NO WAY!"**

The beginning of new knowledge. The following paragraph is a summarization of how my husband and I were given further clarification on my son's condition after being told his primary diagnosis:

"Mr. and Mrs. Bryant, imagine your son living in an apartment building with others who have his diagnosis. All live

13

in the same apartment as they all have the syndrome in common. However, your son is on a floor all by himself. His syndrome and his particular deletion on his gene is like hitting the lottery in a ***bad way***."

For years I couldn't get that parable out of my head—"hitting the lottery in a bad way". I guess to some extent I still can't, but I live with it better. My son, Mason, lives with a rare and complex chromosomal abnormality, which includes a host of anomalies that to this date and time affects approximately 200 individuals in the world. It is called ATRX Syndrome (Alpha Thalessemia X-linked Intellectually Disabled). His cognitive prognosis is severe/profound. He is the **only** individual who is registered with his specific gene mutation in the world thus far. My son is quite a unique individual, but aren't we all? Mason consumes his nutrition to sustain life through a g-tube. He is non-ambulatory and non-verbal. When Mason was five years-old his second diagnosis was revealed as Microscopic Polyangiitis and it positions itself under the Vasculitis disease. He is monitored closely by Rheumotology and Pulmonology as this disease can be life-threatening. Essentially, one's blood vessels burst in the body's organ systems. It varies for each individual. For Mason, his capillary blood vessels burst in his lungs. Before the diagnosis, he was often mistakenly diagnosed with pneumonia, which in his case was blood in his lungs. I cannot count how many times we have heard doctors say, "He is a puzzle," because of his numerous etiopathologies.

The "new normal". My family and I are blessed to have home-health care several hours out of the week that allows us to work, go to school, and attend to the nuances of everyday life. As advocate parents we are responsible for managing health care services for our son. This entails all the hiring, firing, training, scheduling, and operations of a successful business. I could not have completed my Ph. D. without home- health- care services. However, when the nurses' shift ends ours begins. This makes for a punctuated lifestyle. Unpredictable is an understatement, especially if Mason becomes ill.

Day- to- day living. A typical day for Mason involves a full-day of strategic planning with no deviation unless absolutely necessary. He has bolus feeding or water per his g-tube every two hours. Medication may or may not be with some feeding or water. Doctor appointments, physical, occupational, speech therapy, and just having fun being a kid is all methodically worked into a daily schedule of "must do's." Getting off schedule can be hell trying to play catch up at times. This schedule is extremely unnatural when we, the parents, are the main caregivers. It's one thing to care for others who are dependent when it's your job. It's a major mind shift when just living day- to -day but having to perform activities of daily living (ADLs) for a loved one. One begins to realize how the smallest activities such as watching television, reading a book, or going to the store are taken for granted. The caregivers' ADLs become methodically planned.

Schooling. Mason's medical condition makes it very difficult for him to sustain any sort of continuity in school because of his poor immune system. He qualifies to receive special education services because he is identified under the federal disability categories "multiple disabilities" and/or "developmental delays." He qualified to receive Home Instruction. The classroom teacher is required to have a total of five hours in home visits. His home visits are scheduled one hour a day five days a week.

IEP experience. My parent experience with the IEP process can be described as a rollercoaster ride. To be perfectly candid, it has had its ups and downs. My initial experience was not at all pleasant. I was now the deer caught in the headlights that I recalled seeing when I was sitting on the other side as the educator. My husband had inadvertently received the wrong address and was unable to be at the meeting. If I had known what I know now, I would have rescheduled the meeting or they would have had to wait until I called him back to give him the correct address. I was too manic to make the request. All those people—I never remembered an IEP meeting being so huge when I participated as an educator. I thought my son must have some major issues with their findings from his evaluation. It didn't matter that I was an educator with a Masters' Degree in Education. It didn't matter because at that time I was just Mason's Mom. All the knowledge of education I had made no difference when I walked into that room. I could not believe I was actually in the other role as a parent. Did anyone in the meeting feel as I felt when I was an educator? Did anyone care over there on the other side? I was here to face the sentence of where my son would be placed academically and subsequently, in society.

It was close to the feeling I experienced when we were finally given the long awaited two-year medical diagnosis of ATRX Syndrome. It took everything in me not to burst into tears. I kept feeling like I can't believe I'm here. I saw people's mouths moving but I didn't know what they were saying. I literally pinched myself to bring myself back to reality and to revive my educational and mother knowledge. If all other educational knowledge failed, I refused to allow the knowledge I had as Mason's mother be highjacked. I finally pulled myself together, but the derogatory terms I heard to describe my son resonated very loudly. He was eligible for every service because he scored so poorly in every assessment. Not at the time, but in retrospect I took everything personally, as if they had a personal vendetta against Mason and/or me. Was it what was being said, how it was said, or how it was done that made me so resistant? I can honestly say, I have sometimes cried before IEP meetings but always after. I couldn't let them see me sweat or cry. Since my first IEP meeting, I have been prepared like a warrior. I have to go to these meetings armed with strategies and political savvy because I feel as if I am on a battlefield.

I read a lot of material and attend several trainings, sometimes twice, so I can gain the information needed to advocate for Mason. My initial experience was counteracting the constant "no we cannot" response and attitudes that simply meant money and time. My requests for what I thought, and now know, to be better were minute, qualifiable and common sense. For example, extended-year program (EYP) allows a child to make up days during the summer when they are too ill or hospitalized during the school year. Besides, he only received, at that time, less than five hours of Home Instruction. I would remind myself that I wasn't asking for anything he didn't deserve just so I could gain the nerve to request it. I was made to feel like my requests were too astronomical. I had to figure out how to negotiate in and out of the roles of educator and mother. If I was in my mother-role, would they listen versus me in my educator-role? I finally decided to remain in the role of "educated-mother". The mother of a child with an IEP advised me to let the team know I was working on my Ph.D., so that I would get their attention and respect. For me, that wasn't the answer because I wanted them to see, listen, and value me for being Mason's mother. In addition, that would have made me just like some of them--"the authority." Don't get me wrong, when I have to use my "trump card," I do; but only if I feel my professional knowledge is being undermined. I don't have to possess a Ph.D. to have my mother-knowledge that comes innately in some situations and in others from my eight years of experience. Fortunately, most of the time, Mason has received what he needs, but not after a fight. Most of the time, I receive a copy of his IEP plan before the meeting to see if I need to add anything. Initially, I had to request to review the IEP before the actual meeting. I prefer and now still request to read the IEP plan before the actual meeting. My recent experiences with IEP meetings have been comparatively pleasant. I am still trying to make meaning of why my current experience is extraordinarily different. Have I become savvier in my role as mother? Is the staff in this district better equipped to work with special families? Is it because this district's IEP Team meets at the student's home for meetings and this has empowered me and disempowered them?

Power in the individualized educational program. The most important person in the IEP meeting should be the student for whom the IEP is intended, because that is who brings everyone together. Control of the meeting can come from an individual, such as the facilitator, or from the environment. The most powerful individual or entity is the one who can take the challenges and issues raised in the meeting and influence the other IEP team members. Who holds the power at one IEP meeting may change at another, as it is fluid. As a parent who has a child on an IEP, I would like to see more of the adaptive work put into the entire IEP process from beginning to end. Adaptive work is confronting beliefs/ideologies and personal values. Simply put, adaptive work challenges reality as well as heterogeneity versus hegemonic thinking (Heifetz, 1994). I want to experience is my child truly being considered an individual and truly working towards plans that may not be linear but demonstrate continuity of growth.

22

Life beyond the individualized educational program. Mason is not identified by any of his diagnosed conditions. He is fun, loving, personable, and amazing in every aspect. He is quite a ham! I am (constantly, continuously) astonished at his small but consistent progress. There are several challenges a parent such as myself continuously confronts. Being a parent of a child who lives with special needs is an ongoing challenge that never ceases but you learn to adapt to change when it confronts you. I am stricken with great disappointment when I cannot figure out what could be wrong with Mason when he's not feeling well because he is nonverbal. It's a great challenge when individuals and society don't consider his existence. Perhaps the biggest challenge is when Mason is rushed to the Emergency Department (ED) and the thought enters my mind, "Is this it, will he make it this time?" I am never consumed with the thought of Mason's death, but I would not be truthful if I didn't admit the thought does enter my mind every time he has an acute issue. Fortunately, the biggest lesson learned thus far is maintaining perseverance in all aspects of our lives although lessons have been never ending. I cannot conclude without mentioning that there are regularly enjoyable encounters with Mason. In particular, I want to share two. First, when Mason looked at me for the first time rather than look through me, there was a connection that is almost too complicated to describe. It was him speaking to me from the depth of his soul, "I understand, I am with you, I see you Mommy." It was not just the physical act of seeing but the abstract act of seeing me. Second, every time he has awakened from a horrific medical event during a hospital stay with a smile, I have known he would be okay.

Situating Myself as Researcher

Who do I think I am to have the audacious spirit to pursue such revealing material? I have grappled with my desire to pursue this study and finally came to "my" truth that it would be innately impossible to conduct such a study without a mere thought of my own situation. I certainly cannot deny my frontline status of being a mother of a child who lives with severe cognitive delays, who is medically fragile, but who is an experienced educator no more than I can deny the color of my skin, and I do not apologize for my subjectivities. My unique personal experiences will deepen the tension of this study. My personal experiences have also been the premise for much needed work in the special education field and my aspiration to seek out like parents. Being cognizant of the contextual complexities and inescapable subjectivity, I have chosen to be transparent, to liberate my silent thoughts and allow my voice to be heard, hopefully as an echo to other parents' narratives.

My Insider/Outsider Positionality

The dialectic relationship between insider/outsider positioning is a balancing act that commits me to being transparent. My advantages of possessing an insider/outsider positionality is as equal as the reasons for the disadvantages. As an insider I am privy to the nuances of this life style. As an outsider I must consciously practice not to assume a parent's response. Insider/outsider positionality should challenge one to interrogate their thoughts appropriately. My insider/outsider positionality enhances this body of work as it is continuously fluid, fluent and relevant. Fluid is not fixed it moves or changes appropriately. Fluent as I am self-assured that self-introspect will keep me centered. Relevancy is applicable because one position, i.e., insider or outsider is always present.

CHAPTER 2: LITERATURE REVIEW

Introduction

      This literature review will offer a brief and general review of the history of the Individualized Education Program (IEP) and what knowledge and ideas have been established and researched regarding parents' rights and roles on the team in their child's IEP. In addition, a review of empirical studies that represent positive/satisfied or negative/dissatisfied parent experiences with their child's IEP. Then it takes an account of mediating factors that question the power asymmetries and how meaningful parental participation could be the glue that seals the longevity of a collaborative relationship within the special education sphere and IEP process. Finally, the topic is broadened to areas beyond the IEP experience for parents and their children who live with special needs.

IEP History and Qualifications

      The evolution of the IEP is rooted in legal struggle to ensure that all students receive equal educational opportunity. A student qualifies for an IEP after an extensive evaluation of all areas of

27

concern that may qualify as a disability and would benefit from special education and special services. The evaluation includes existing information about the child's issues and additional concerns to assist in making a determination. With the parents' permission, other qualified professionals, tests, observations, and medical records are considered. A meeting is held and eligibility is determined once a child is identified with one or more disabilities that qualifies them for specialized education services. The Individuals with Disabilities Education Act (IDEA) provides a definition of what qualifies as a disability. There are 13 different categories of disabilities that define a qualifying disability for a child to be eligible for special education and services. The following provides a short definition of each disability: 1.) Autism: Delays affecting communication and social interactions. Additional characteristics are repetitive movements and resistance to change in environments or daily routine; 2.) Deaf-blindness: hearing and visual impairments; 3.) Deafness: hearing impairment; 4.) Emotional disturbance: unstable emotional status that acutely affects educational performance; 5.) Hearing impairment: permanent or fluctuating impairment in hearing; 6.) Intellectual disability:

significant intellectual delay; 7.) Multiple disability: Concomitant

impairments; 8.) Orthopedic: severe orthopedic impairment; 9.) Other

health impairment: restricted or heightened health issues that impedes

learning; 10.) Specific learning disability: learning disorder that affects

the comprehension of language, written or spoken; 11.) Speech or

language impairment: communication disorder such as stuttering or

voice impairment; 12.) Traumatic brain injury: external injury to the

brain resulting in cognitive, memory, speech, physical and emotional

impairments; 13.) Visual impairment: impairment of vision that

includes partial and blindness (http://nichcy.org/disability/categories

March 2012).

Part B of the Individuals with Disabilities Education Act

(IDEA) is formerly known as Education for All Handicapped Children

Act (Public Law 94-142). IDEA mandates that school systems must

ensure that every effort has been made for parents to participate in the

IEP and that they are made fully aware of the IEP, and that they

comprehend results even in the absence of being physically present at the child's Individual Education Program conferences. Part B essentially speaks to the notion that parents are fully engaged in the IEP process from notification of the IEP meeting to the comprehension of the discussion within the meeting and any information disseminated as well as alternative accommodations in the event the parent cannot be present (Individuals with Disabilities Education Act, 1997 Sec. 300.322 Parent participation).

An IEP is a legal document that articulates several required components. The IEP must include the student's present levels of educational performance and information regarding how the student's disability impedes their involvement and progress in the general curriculum. It is also required to define measurable goals and objectives. The IEP document drives the student's special educational program. Huefner (2000) describes the IEP as the blueprint of the student's educational career.

The "Centerpiece"

Envisioning the IEP as the centerpiece of the statute's education delivery system for disabled children, and aware that schools had all too often denied such children appropriate educations without in any way consulting their parents, Congress repeatedly emphasized throughout the Act the importance and indeed the necessity of parental participation in both the development of the IEP and any subsequent assessment of its effectiveness. Honig v. Doe, 484 U.S. 305, 1988 (Wright & Wright, 2007, p. 370)

Parental Rights Within Individual Education Process

Parents have always been viewed as members of the Individualized Education Program since its inception in 1975 by the Education for All Handicapped Children Act, now known as Individuals with Disabilities Education Act (IDEA). However, in 1997 with the passage of Public Law 94-142 (P.L. 94-142) reauthorizing the IDEA, it mandated that school systems must ensure parental participation in the IEP and that they are made fully aware of the process and comprehend results even in the absence of their physical presence at the child's Individualized Education Program conferences. Unfortunately, P. L. 94-142 was not explicit in explaining parental participation—what does realistic parent participation mean and how is it measured? In other words, school systems can be in compliance with simply the presence of parents but meaningful participation could very well be absent (Flanigan, 2007). Parents who are unaware of their rights within the IEP often find themselves in a role of passivity and tend to accept the cultural practices of the school. In other words, parents who are inadequately prepared in the knowledge of their rights could easily be coerced and seduced into agreeing.

IEP's Roles and Team Process

Parents, of course, have valuable knowledge regarding their children. Hence, their participation in the IEP process is a valuable part of a comprehensive IEP plan. Although many parents may not have the expertise to analyze educational evaluation data, they may nevertheless possess knowledge that can enhance their child's academic approach (Dabkowski, 2004). Among the lengthy issues of developing an effective and legally abiding IEP, is the complexity of the roles and team process dated before the parental participation under the passage of P.L. 94-142 in 1997 to date. Yoshida and Gottlieb (1977) argue that parents appear to be on the sideline as opposed to being a valued key player that participates and contributes throughout the child's IEP process. In a survey disseminated among professional school planning team members, it was felt that parents' roles should be limited to gathering and presenting information to their child's case versus participating in the educational planning (Lusthaus & Lusthaus and Gibbs, 1981; Lytle and Bordin, 2001). According to Yoshida and Gottlieb (1977) parents assume the role of "passive participant" (p. 17). This assumed role may have been the result of school professional practices. According to Goldstein, Strickland, Turnbull, and Curry's (1980) study, in seven scenarios the IEPs had been written with predetermined goals and parents where only asked for their approval. According to Gilliam and Coleman (1981), parents feel like they are on the receiving side of information rather than being major contributing members. Parents are concerned that recommendations

for services were predetermined (Turnbull and Leonard, 1981). This

causes parents to feel left out, disempowered, and devalued (National

Council on Disability, 1995). Families felt that pre-determined goals

created an environment that was not conducive to their becoming true

participants in the process. Simon (2006) argues that these sort of

practices leads to untrustworthiness and frustration when a key

member is not being acknowledged equally. In a recent study that

investigated a preference of whether families prefer customary IEP

meetings versus a Student Centered Individualized Education Planning

(SCIEP) led by Childre and Chambers (2005), these families believed

that their role in traditional IEP meetings was to only listen to

information and answer questions. These families favored the SCIEP

approach because it fostered an environment of dual in-depth

communication about relative concerns. Indeed professional practices

that disregard parents' input substantiate the charge of IEPs being

predetermined, confusing and emitting mechanical characteristics

(Banks and Banks, 2005). In other words, for parents, IEPs can be appear superficial, status quo and inflexible.

Empirical Studies of Parents' Experiences with IEP's

The following empirical studies will illustrate positive/satisfied and negative/dissatisfied parents' experiences during the Individual Education Program process. This will include but not be limited to parents' experiences within the IEP meeting and the entire process within the special education realm. According to the empirical studies viewed in this research (Flanagan, 2001), there is a gulf between positive/satisfied and negative/dissatisfied experiences of the parents during the process determining their child's Individual Education Program. Parents still feel after two decades of implementation of IDEA and passage of Public Law 94-142 in 1997 that they are not equal active participants (Flanigan,2007). The following paragraphs will demonstrate the most popular stances parents took away from their experience with IEP's, i.e. positive/satisfied, negative/dissatisfied and mixed experiences. I will offer an analysis of all postures in the conclusion of this sub-section explaining the possible reasons for such experiences.

Parents' Negative/Dissatisfied Experience

In an early study, The National Council of Disability (1995) received complaints in over 400 testimonies from families of children living with special needs who reported their dissatisfaction with IEP process; they suggested that the outcomes were predetermined and thus parental participation was not needed. Practices of this nature leave parents feeling "disenfranchised and alienated from educational systems designed to help their children" (Kroth & Edge, 1997 p.14).

Flanigan's (2007) concluded that after 25 years (at the time the research was conducted) of the inception of the Individuals with Disabilities Education Act in 1997 (IDEA) the process of special education evaluation is a disappointment for parents who have children living with special needs. Parents lack the knowledge of the process and do not feel like equal participants.

Fish (2008) conducted a study that found that parents of children living with autism described their first IEP experiences to be negative. His research findings included the following: parents did not perceive themselves as being equal; parents believed their input was not valued; the IEP document lacked proper protocol; objectives stated in the IEP meetings were not followed through and those parents new to special education had issues with comprehending the special education laws and were not cognizant of services available for their children. Interestingly, when staff attended the IEP meetings for support to these parents, the proper professional protocol behavior was followed. Concluding this study, Fish pointed out that despite the adversarial relationship between parents and school officials things did improve after educational awareness of both parents and educators. Similarly, Stoner, Bock, Thompson, Angell, Heyl and Crowley (2005) interviewed married couples of children who lived with autism spectrum disorder (ASD). The married couples believed their experience of their first IEP process to be everything but comprehensible and illustrated attitudes of dissatisfaction.

As reported in the research, even school officials feel overwhelmed by the special education process. For instance, Steve

McKee (2004) talks about his first experience with special education and how he was taken aback by its less than perfect representation of "special education". He described it as an unexpected lifestyle punctuated with intricate procedures, perplexing documentation and encrypted jargon (p. 39). Like McKee, O'Donovan (2007) affirms feelings of entering a maze of mysterious dealings undergirded with hysteria. O'Donovan is a director of family support for a school district. He is candid about how school administration and staff have become so engrossed with the details of IEP's that they lose sight and forget how this could appear from a parent's perspective in special education. The IEP meetings usually include several school staff members, which may make the parent feel outnumbered. This is followed by parents having to make sense of convoluted federal laws and mandates which are obscure even for educators to understand. O'Donovan also acknowledges that the emotions of a parent of a child who lives with special needs goes beyond the IEP setting in having to deal with the day- to -day tasks. In his article, he speaks of school districts moving in the right direction to reach out to parents with less adversarial methods and thinking out of the box. However, one district's primary focus in their IEPs is driven by legal compliancy versus student. The influx of due process hearings and arbitrations may be the source spearheading such a theory (O'Donovan, 2007). However, this questions the ethical measures in making transformations within the special education field. Do we change because it hurts our pockets rather than because we hurt the very, families who intend to help in the first place?

In a study conducted by M. Janus, L. Kopechanski, R. Cameron and D. Huges (2008) concluded that 40 parent participants of four to six year-old children living with special needs had unsatisfactory results at the transitional status (pre-school to kindergarten) even in a current climate of support. The authors feel ineffective policies that lack communication and a connectedness with available resources had plenty to do with such outcomes.

Parents' Positive/Satisfied Experience

Beth A. Jones (2006) conducted a study that involved a mini-conference intervention before the actual IEP meeting to determine if parent participation would increase. A mini-conference is held between the parents and special education teachers before the IEP meeting where the parents are informed of their child's competencies and are encouraged to collaborate on the proposed IEP. Jones' (2006) study revealed that although there was no difference in parent participation, there was an increase in the level of satisfaction of the parents with their experience due to the mini-conference intervention. This study also aimed to determine whether or not the disability of the child and the socio-economic-status of the family had an effect on the parent participation in IEP meetings. According to the study's findings there was no evidence to support this.

In a survey conducted by Wade Fish (2008), for middle- to upper-middle class participants who were white, non-Hispanic overall positive IEP experiences. The 51 participants where parents of students receiving special education services from a family support service center. Participants felt their input into IEP meetings to be valued; they were treated with respect and saw themselves as part of the decision making team. In addition, most of the parents reported they had a clear understanding of the IEP process and special education law. The purpose of this study was to determine reasons that increase the belief that parents felt IEP meetings were serving their children appropriately.

Michelle Diament (2012) reported results in her article about parents' experiences with their child's IEP. It was posted on "Disability Scoop", a resource website for parents with children who live with special needs, titled "Most Parents Pleased with Role in Child's IEP." The study measured the experiences of over 10,000 families who attended their child's IEP meetings. Seventy percent of these parents claim their level of participation in decision- making was satisfactory.

Parents' Variegated Experiences

As clear as there are parents who are unequivocal that their experience was either positive/satisfied or negative/dissatisfied with their IEP process, there are parents who are ambivalent. This is neither good nor bad. It demonstrates and affirms for this research the possibilities among parents' experiences within the special education sphere.

For example, a national study conducted by Public Agenda (2002) did a random telephone survey between April 12 and May 11, 2002 involving 510 interviews of special education principals, superintendents and parents of public- school- age children living with special needs. Of these 510 interviewed, most principals and superintendents gave their own schools' special education programs satisfactory ratings. However, among these surveys a marginal amount of parents experienced frustrating bureaucratic tactics as well as some parents having to fight just to get their children the services they needed. It is important to note that three focus groups and four in-depth interviews involved parents and 13 in-depth interviews involved special education authorities such as principals and superintendents.

In Diament's (2012) study, although the greater response was positive, there were other parents who were dissatisfied with the IEP. Among those dissatisfied were those parents whose children were identified with difficult behavior or social skills. Comparably, race and social-economic status seem to play a role with those who were white and had higher income levels purporting to have had better experience than those from opposite demographic groups.

According to Goldberg's (2012) study, responding to Diaments's (2012) study, about two million parents are unsatisfied but are not doing anything about it. Some of the reasons for parent dissatisfaction are as follows: 1.) Some schools make parents feel that there will be irreparable harm to the parent-school relationship if they file for some form of dispute resolution, 2.) Some parents are overwhelmed by the process and just don't know how to proceed, 3.) Even though parents can get reimbursed for legal fees if they win a due process complaint, they currently cannot get reimbursed for expert witness fees. It can be difficult to win a Due Process Hearing without expert witnesses, and 4.) There is a lot of misinformation about the Dispute Resolution process under IDEA provided to parents.

These factors that inhibit parent complaints are important because school districts use the low percentage of due process complaints as evidence of satisfied parents (Goldberg, 2012).

According to Goldberg (2012), this is simply not the case.

Analysis of Empirical Studies of Parents' Experiences

There are a host of reasons as to why there are variations in parents' experiences with special education. Again, this current study was conducted to reveal parents' stories of their experiences during their child's IEP process. Bruce C. Caines (1998) discovered that both positive and negative attitudes of school authorities towards parents and their children who live with disabilities were the most influential aspect affecting the IEP. Parents in Caines' (1998) study felt that they had to contend with attitude barriers, which were the greatest hindrance for gaining an IEP for their children. Attitude barriers are those negative behaviors and approaches that present obstacles for progression. The attitudes were more daunting than the inexperience of school personnel in the development of IEPs. However, the attitudes were specific to individuals and not to the entire school or district.

Susan Ladd Latham (2002) identified the lack of knowledge parents have about navigating appropriate sources for support, which creates a fluctuating feeling from optimistic and trusting to pessimistic and suspicion. The appropriate communication, knowledge and information of resources are monumental in the initial years for parents of children who are in special education. The lack of this sort of communication could discourage parent involvement and positive/satisfied experiences for parents during these initial years of special education.

Even though the Public Agenda's study (2002) found that most participants gave high ratings to their schools, there was a minority of parents who were frustrated as they continued to contend with unhelpful and a disobliging bureaucracy. The demographics for this frustrated population of parents were not stated in this study. The sample of participants was taken from a national random telephone survey of 510 parents of K-12 public schools where the children were identified with specific learning disabilities, ADD or ADHD, speech or language impairment, mental retardation or emotional disturbance, hearing or vision impairment, autism, or other disabilities. Sixteen percent of these frustrated parents wanted to take their schools to court, 38% said their children would perform better if they had better teachers, 39% said their child's special education program was inadequate and needs improvement; 35% were frustrated with just getting the services their child needed; and 33% said the school was doing a fair or poor job assisting their child. Since this study was conducted in public school districts, one could speculate that the frustrated minority of parents might fall in various demographics, i.e. race, parent education level, and socio-economic status. Public Agenda's study (2002) found that

70 % of these parents felt that their children living with special needs are not getting services because their parents are not aware of the resources available. Whose responsibility is it to inform parents of resources that are available…parent or school? Interestingly enough, 55 % say it is the responsibility of the parent to research such resources because "the school is not going to volunteer the information" (p.2). (It was not clear who made this statement.) The following was a parent's experience with the school psychologist from Public Agenda study (2002): "You know what (he) told me?" He said,

46

'If you weren't so persistent, I wouldn't give you these services." (p. 3). If this is the experience of even a small percentage of parents, this should not be acceptable on any level.

Beth A. Jones (2006) study revealed although there was no difference in parent participation, there was an increase in the level of satisfaction of the parents IEP experience due to the mini-conference intervention. She also observed these parents to be passive participants in their role as equal members.

Race and socio-economic status may have had an impact on the overwhelming positive outcome of Fish's (2008) study. Eighty percent of his parent participants' race and class positions are ones of privilege and therefore felt less threatened by the IEP process. The parent participants felt their experiences were positive, believed education authorities valued their contributions, treated them with respect, and saw them as equal decision- making members.

Perhaps another contributing factor for these conflicting outcomes may be the varying disabilities that qualify a child for having an IEP. In other words, a parent whose child has been identified with "multiple disabilities" may have a totally different experience from that parent whose child has been identified with "orthopedic impairment." Likewise, parents of varying education level, socio- economic status, and race may also have very different experiences as suggested in previous studies (Martin, Marshall, & Sale, 2004; Turnbull & Turnbull, 2001; Fish, 2008, Diament, 2012; Valle, 2009).

Processing Power in the Individualized Education Process

The silence of parents' voices is so loud that no one can hear. There is an obvious absence of the voice of the parents who might express their experiences in the IEP process. The following sections discuss research that shows the many reasons why we don't hear parents' voices in the IEP process. This section will highlight some of the possible silencing structures that may impede the voice of parents who have children who live with special needs and have an IEP within our school systems.

Ruling Ideologies in the Individual Education Process

While it is the spirit of the law's intentions to allow parents to serve as equal members of the IEP team, the perpetual resistance from parents and their outright cries of disparity is a resounding indicator

that something needs to be examined and addressed. In other words,

the implementation of parent and school collaboration is important, but

the fundamentals of interrogating practices, of being proactive in our

actions and in seeking continual feedback from parents are paramount.

Without these sincere deliberate efforts the IEP movement is

"motionless" and is nothing more than an idea on paper that sounds

and looks like progression.

Christopher C. Plum (2008) discovered a discrepancy between policy

and practices within the IEP process. Plum studied the interactions

within the IEP meetings by observing the interaction between the

school psychologist and the parents of children on IEPs. His analysis

confirms the disproportionate distribution of power within this

relationship and space. Using the conversation- analysis method Plum

(2008) concluded that both school psychologist and parent were in

deeply embedded roles. The parents assumed the role of passivity,

which gave consent for the school psychologist to take control of the

future of their child's individual educational program. Plum argues this interaction is far from the collaborative premise of P.L. 94-142. His research revealed that the readings of the diagnostic results were pre-determined readings given by the school psychologist. "The meetings are supposed to be collaborative, but are really driven by the diagnostic results and the school psychologist's power. There's a clear gap between policy and practice," (Plum, 2008). Valle (2009) witnessed similar asymmetries in her tenure as a parent advocate. Quite often she witnessed coercive- persuasion practices from authorities in education disguised in a manner of collaboration in the name of parental advocacy. There was an obvious imbalance in power as many times school authorities display their hierarchal knowledge during meetings as they control the flow, language, and environment. Having their children described in terms of perplex test scores and shortfalls has left many parents with feelings of despair. Valle (2009) recalled seeing these very same parents (mothers) crying in the school parking lot while school personnel, from the same meeting, regarded the meeting successful.

In a rare and much needed contribution, Valle (2009) conducted a collective narrative inquiry and critical-discourse analysis from a chronology of mothers from various backgrounds from the 1960's to the present. Her progressive study examines and demonstrates through the authentic voices of mothers the undeniable similarities of continued issues and how we, today, might go about challenging ethical practices within special education. Juxtaposing past and present practices establishes a strong argument to seek new thinking in addressing mechanical practices as well as acknowledging and continuing progressive movements. An illustration of new thinking and progressive movement would be the implementation of the P.L. 94-142/ 300.322 parent participation laws. The law resonates as a great and much needed augmentation to the IDEA. However, Brueggemann (1999) warns us that history, although valuable, may portray the "official" illusion of progressiveness. Some historical events may be coopted perspectives of those other than individuals who actually have the lived experience, i.e., *about* the people but not *of* the people. "In much of the research literature around parents, research is conceptualized as research *on* parents **rather** than research *with* parents. Research thus presents researchers' *stories of parents*, **rather** than *parents' stories.*"(J. Clandinin, D. Pushor and Murray Orr, 2007, p. 30).

In Valle's (2009) conclusion, she asks school authorities to consider:

Evidence of our conscious or unconscious oppression of mothers lies within their resistance to our practices— for there is no resistance without the presence of power. As revealed within the narratives of mothers, resistance takes place in multiple forms at the local level where power is exercised. We must pay attention to the "special cases" and their points of resistance—for it is within such resistances that we see the unintended consequences of our practices.

If we are to ever to achieve the kind of collaboration with parents envisioned under the law, we must be willing to let go of our expert stance to consider other equally valid "ways of know." I contend that we can move closer to parents only by embracing their subjectivity (p. 222).

School vs. Medical Model

The special education discourse can isolate and persuade parents to conform to a "medical model" mentality. Obscure terms and intentions to frame a pathology leaves parents to accept educational professionals as the only authority to their child's educational future (A. Harris, 2010; Valle, 2009). Valle (2009) compares "the medical model" as an illustration of special education practices. For example, she writes,

A patient (student) presents with symptoms (educational problems). An expert (school psychologist) performs an examination (psycho-educational assessment) to make or rule out a diagnosis (disability). If there is a disability, a prescription (individualized education plan [IEP]) is written with a recommendation for a course of treatment (special

education placement and individual instruction) as well

as a follow-up plan (yearly IEP review). In other words,

special education meetings often function as a means to

inform parents about test results, diagnoses, and

proposed treatment. This scenario reproduces our

cultural norms for a conventional doctor/patient

relationship—precluding the kind of collaboration

envisioned under law. (p. xiv)

Depending on the severity of the child's medical condition,

parents may be disenfranchised in the medical arena as well (Turnbull

& Turnbull, 2001). This goes without mention of the assumed role of

"passive participant" in the presence of medical professionals. This

continuous recurrence of conjecture is on-going beyond the IEP

process. "It is hard to believe that a family thrust into such a horrific

vortex of medical and financial uncertainty must also fight for their

child's schooling" (Bessell, 2001 p. 44).

Education, Race, and Social-Economic Vagaries in Parents' Experiences

To date, research continues to posit conflicting parental attitudes towards the IEP process. However, research is consistent with an overabundance of documentation of parent participants being more dissatisfied than satisfied. Studies (Argus-Calvo, B., Tafoya, N.G., & L. L., 2005; Beth Harry, 2008; B. Harry, 1992) suggest there are cultural and linguistic barriers that hinder a fair and successful experience. This includes meager interpretation services, and feelings of not being valued and being marginalized and disenfranchised. According to Rock (2000), barriers include attitudes, cultural background, logistics, and parental responsibilities. Schools must be successful in making reasonable accommodations such as environment, cultural, and language. "Parents who are supported in their initial attempts to participate in decision making will likely continue these efforts later in their child's school career" (Dabkowski, 2004, p.38). Cultural differences are not only race and ethnic differences, but also varying understandings of perception of disability. For instance, there are some cultures that believe it is disrespectful to disagree with school officials as well as cultures that believe that disability is of supernatural intent (Lamorey, 2002 and Whitebread, Burder, Fleming & Park, 2007)

It has also been suggested that parents' economic, education, and social status has a correlation to a lack of parental participation (Witt, Miller, McIntyre & Smith, 1984; Winters, 1993; Harris, 2010). There are conflicting research studies that indicate a parent's level of education determines the degree of IEP participation, such as asking questions, offering input, and being comfortable in the IEP meetings (Jones, 2006; Witt, Miller, McIntyre & Smith, 1984; Lynch & Stein, 1982).

Meaningful Family Participation and Involvement

The term "meaningful" used in this current research speaks to the depth of participation and involvement i.e., parents' views and feelings are implemented into the decision making process of the IEP. A parent from the 2007 "Partners in Policy-making' course made the following comment:

Building parents' views and preferences into the commissioning, the planning systems—and the need to remember that "one size fits all" is wrong for families with disabled children. We are all different (as cited in Philippa Russell, 2008).

Parental involvement of children who live with disabilities increases the advancement of their child's academics, hence Individual Education Program (Turnbull & Turnbull, 2001; Spann, Kohler, & Soenksen, 2003; Russell, 2008). Parental involvement fosters the following benefits:

1. Increase the teacher's understanding of the child's environment.

2. Add to parents' knowledge of the child's educational setting.

3. Improve communication between parents and the school.

4. Increase the school's understanding of the child.

5. Increase the likelihood that, with improved understanding between home and school, mutually agreed upon educational goals will be attained.

(Smith, 2006)

Since school systems appear to be pre-occupied with other matters, they lack the practice of building and sustaining relationships with parents from the onset of the IEP process. Hammond, Ingall and Trussell (2008) contend that educators need to be cognizant of the possible responses parents may experience in the initial stages of the IEP process. Hammond, Ingall, and Trussell, (2008) interviewed 212 parents during a course of four years. One of the several concerns expressed by parents was that the IEP meetings should implement a framework that encourages more opportunities for meaningful parental involvement. So that their concerns would be known and included in the agenda, parents should be involved in the planning stage before the actually IEP meeting occurs. Patricia Sheehey (2006) conducted a case study of the experiences of three Hawaiian parents and their role in the decision making for their children's IEPs. According to Sheehey

(2006), data analysis revealed three significant findings in parents'
experiences in educational decision-making. First, the parents'
definition of "involvement" in educational decision-making wasn't
congruent to that of the legal term. Second, advocacy was the driving
force behind involvement for the parents in this case study. Lastly, the
parents in this case study displayed resistance when they were
presented with finished IEPs at the IEP meeting.

Staples and Diliberto (2010) explain the fundamentals of
parental involvement that is essential for parent-teacher collaboration--
building parent rapport, developing a communication system with a
maintenance plan, and creating additional special event opportunities
for parent involvement. Bridging these perspectives could be
monumental in the initial formatting of the IEP process. "Building
positive parent and teacher relationships is time consuming; however,
it is essential for the optimal success of the child" (Staples and
Diliberto, 2010, p. 63). This type of collaborative model building
promotes optimistic outcomes one of which includes the planning of
the child's IEP (Staples and Diliberto, 2010). A collaborative system

should be continuous before and after the IEP process. Thus, the parent can sustain a feeling of team decision-making and a sense of trust. Valle (2011) argues for a plurality of methodological frameworks that will create a movement of addressing difficult questions. These difficult questions is "adaptive work" Heifetz (2004) that challenges us to make a shift in values, behaviors, beliefs and roles. Adaptive work is well over due in our American Special Education System.

A Parent's Life Experience Beyond the IEP Experience

Living with special needs doesn't begin for the parent and child with the individualized education program (IEP) in the academic domain of special education. The IEP is just another chapter, phase, or dimension of their lives. Thinking of what real life experiences may be like for these families beyond the IEP process has not been part of the traditional way schools have practiced in terms of academic services. Schools need to consider the numerous experiences these families have beyond the IEP process in order to get a broader perspective and understanding.

Day-to-Day Living Raising a Child Who Lives with Special Needs

The term "special needs" refers to the ever growing collection of developmental disabilities that can affect an individual's way of independent living. This involves activities of daily living (ADLs) that most individuals take for granted such as seeing, walking, eating, talking and communicating, hearing, thinking and cognitive ability, climbing, and caring for oneself (Hildebrand 2000, S. Schultz 2011). The term "medically fragile" refers to, but is not limited to, the following: Enteral Feeding Tube, Total Parenteral Feeding, Cardiorespiratory Monitoring Intravenous, Therapy Ventilator dependent, Oxygen Support, Urinary Catherization, Renal Dialysis Ministrations imposed by tracheotomy, colostomy, Ileostomey and conditions that are deteriorating and which may cause injury or death (Admin_MedFrag Tuesday, 13 April, 2010 http://medicallyfragilechild.com/medically-fragile-child-definition/) .

Raising a typical growing child and a child living with special needs certainly have commonalities such as maintaining day-to-day work and family activities. However, to think that the day- to- day living when raising a child who lives with special needs is equivalent to raising a typical child couldn't be further from the truth. Include medically fragile to the special needs equation and the situation can become exponentially challenging. Williamson (2011) says there are realistic attributes and major differences such as costly stresses and burdens with raising children who live with special needs versus those who are typically developing. However, I'm not sure if people really know all the nuances that can sometimes accompany a hectic, methodical, and challenging regime that comes with the daily duties of raising a child who lives with special needs and/or is medically fragile (Annemarie C. Tadema and Carla Vlaskamp, 2009). There are usually no trial runs with getting prepared for raising a child with special needs as many families may not know of the child's special condition until they are born. This can lead to deep emotional stresses (Duttenhoffer, 2010). These stresses are costly and burdensome and may not only create financial burdens, but create social and work life challenges as well.

The complexity of a child's disability can command your attention for an entire day, including the night, as many children who live with special needs are not good sleepers. For instance, a child who is totally dependent, meaning they are incontinent, cannot walk, talk, wash, dress or eat by themselves will command attention at least every two hours. These situations may also include close monitoring for those children who have untimely acute issues such as seizures, tracheostomy care, and gastronomy care. This also includes parents having to use their physical abilities to change positions, moving their child from one part of the room to another room (Mencap, 2001). Then, administrating medication, doctor visits, therapy visits, stimulating and engaging the child all within a day's duration. Finally, there are the duties of what the parents must do aside from the daily recurring duties of day-to-day life such as the on-going telephone calls to schedule doctors' appointments, fighting with insurance companies, advocating for your child, paperwork and bills. Tadema and Vlaskamp (2009) found that of 133 parents of children with intellectual and multiple disabilities (PIMD) most of their children are totally dependent on them for meeting all their basic needs during every hour of the day including night-time. In addition to the day-to-day routine, school issues bring on its on challenges. The previously mentioned events in some cases are permanent for parents (Tadema &Vlaskamp, 2009). "We change our jobs; change our habits; change our manner of dress; change our goals; change our expectation of life; change our dreams; change our relationships; and change our way of thinking when we have a child with special needs…it will change the family" (Williamson, 2011 pg. 2).

The "New Normal" Life

Learning the initial news of your child's living with special needs can be much like dealing with death as all your dreams and admirations for this child could be totally lost (S. Schultz, 2011). It may also resemble Valle's (2011) "Down the Rabbit Hole: A Commentary About Research on Parents and Special Education" in which she metaphorically compares the narratives of 15 mothers entrance to the world of special education to Alice's entrance to Wonderland. She illustrates how Alice's entrance into this mysterious space consistently challenges her sense of making meaning of uncharted surroundings and characters. Both clever and simple, this notion allows anyone who knows the story a common understanding of what it could be like for some parents to enter into the world of special education. Additionally, Valle is impressed by the similarities in the mother's narratives more so than their individualized specifics. This she argues is a unified outcry of issues within our districts that demand our attention beyond a certain stakeholder e.g. child, parent, educator etc… that persistently carriers the same storyline over decades (p. 185).

The process of accepting the news and embracing the situation can take years for some parents. The stress of parents who have children living with disabilities can vary. Fathers and mothers differ in how they cope with stress (Hassal et al. 2005; Islam, Shanaz and Farjana, 2001). Families who seek healthy coping approaches such as spirituality and family and group support they appear to move forward in their lives. Even though confronted with new normal challenges, they utilize their resources to forge ahead. Those parents who don't practice healthy coping strategies can experience enduring stress that not only impacts that parent but the entire family (Tadema & Vlaskamp, 2009; J.J. Binger; Krauss, 2000; Islam MZ, Shanaz R. and Farjana S., 2013). The stressors appear to be never ending. Parents, especially mothers, of children who live with mental retardation experience significantly greater stress than parents who do not have children who live with mental retardation (Islam, Shanaz, Farjana, 2013). Although debunked from recent studies, Michelle Cottie (2012) argues that the commonly stated statistic of 80% of parents of children with autism end in divorce because it feels true for her and her parent friends. A 2009 study found that mothers of children living with autism have stress related hormone cortisol compared to the levels found in combat soldiers and those who suffer from post-traumatic-stress disorder (PTSD) (http://www.ncbi.nlm.nih.gov/pmc/articles/PMC2837763/).

Experiencing disconnection and isolation are very common for parents who have been thrown into the throes of a "new normal" life which is filled with unknowns such as medical jargon, school

66

terminology, and uncomfortable stares from others (G. Gallagher and P. Konjoian, 2010). Schultz (2011) describes how people ignore a mother and her daughter with special needs because the people do not know how to respond. Furthermore, a mother states that the most uncomfortable feeling is knowing they are visible to people but are treated as though they are invisible.

Maria Lin (2012) eloquently describes seven things people don't know about parents of children who live with special needs. I paraphrase her lived experiences as a mother of a son who lives with special needs because it echoes the experiences of so many parents.

1. There is a tiredness that parents of children who live with special needs experience almost constantly; it's not just physical but mental fatigue.

2. The jealousy of seeing typically developing children the same as your child or younger progressing naturally. Even feeling jealousy of other children living with special needs when their disorders are more common and understood.

3. Feeling alone with the honor of being the only one who knows how to care for your special child.

4. Being afraid of the unknowns such as neglect of treatment or diagnosis. Also, the unknowns of the possibilities for what the future holds. People using terms such as "retarded," "short bus," "as long as it's healthy" (referring to their unborn child). These terms are rude and hurtful to the children and their parents who love and nurture them.

5. Parents of children who live with special needs are "Human." The ways that they are pushed and challenged in their "new normal" world may make them react in certain ways...they're only human.

6. The challenges of talking about their children. Sharing about their children can be the most wonderful thing at times because of their child's accomplishments that others may take for granted. Sometimes sharing is overwhelming when their child's diagnosis is complex.

In conclusion I would like to end with a parent's voice that echoes the sub-section of Chapter II "A Parents' Life Experience Beyond the IEP Experience." This essay addresses a school official's question as to why there is a low representation of parents of children who live with special needs involved with local PTA meetings and other issues that effect this population of children. A mother who knows the life of raising a child who lives with special needs vividly captures the sometimes daily painful trials and tribulations in an essay, "Where are the Parents?" (See Appendix A).

Resiliency: Happiness Despite the Circumstances

What does happiness look like in the world of a parent who raises a child who lives with special needs? It looks pretty much the same as a parent raising a typically developing child. For example, a mother shares how her daughter who lives with special needs received her first prom dress in the form of a new wheelchair. It was fuchsia with a green seat cushion. The story behind this odd sounding vignette is that this hard working mom vacillated over the decision to join her husband, a stay at home father, and their daughter to choose a wheelchair at the clinic appointment. She compares this wheelchair choice as picking out a prom dress as there are several decisions that are involved such as how long the child actually spends time in the chair, will it fit and how does it compliment the child. These are the BIG decisions other folks just have no clue about. The mother had to meet with clients so she reluctantly missed this milestone for her daughter. One can imagine the smiles from these proud parents as their daughter received her first "prom dress" (E. Moore, 2010). Parents of children who live with special needs can take the smallest events and make a grand ordeal of it because for them their child accomplished something. Parents are just proud of their children! Consider the following mother's thoughts:

"The world may perceive us as being unhappier than other parents. And yes, we may very well have more pressures and stress. But the truth is, we get just as much bliss in our children as other parents do from theirs. They may have special needs, but they are not "defective." They are out children. In fact, our happiness can be that much greater because our kids work so hard for their achievements. The first steps my son took at age 3 weren't just milestones—they were miracles" (E. Seidman, 2013 Mar 19).

"Raising a child with any disorder, condition or special need, is both a blessing and a challenge. A challenge for the obvious reasons, and a blessing because you don't know the depths of victory and joy until you see your child overcoming some of those challenges sometimes while smiling like a goofy bear" (Marie Lin, 2012).

CHAPTER 3: METHODOLOGY

Introduction

I chose phenomenological narrative inquiry for my methodological approach because phenomenology aims to comprehend and describe the lived experiences of individuals, not to explain or analyze (Moustakas, 1994). The process is not necessarily seeking the answer as much as it is the process of bringing the topic and information into circulation to the possibilities and perhaps provide *Verstehen* (understanding). Narrative inquiry not only permitted me to capture the experiences of parents during their child's Individual Education Process (IEP), but it also illuminated the heartfelt power of their reflective accounts. Relationships of trust and longevity are created through these outlets of personal experiences making it easier for unearthing an oppressed voice (Butler-Kisber, 2010). The phrase "narrative as the human enterprise" delineates for me the closest others can get to embodying the experience of the storyteller (Butler-Kisber, 2010, p. 52). Laurel Richardson also provides an important insight into the importance of narrative:

If we wish to understand the deepest and most

universal of human experiences, if we wish our work to

be faithful to the lived experiences of people, if we

wish for a union between poetics and science, or if we

wish to use privileges and skills to empower the people

we study, then we *should* value the narrative

(Richardson, 1995, pp. 218-219).

Norman Denzin and Yvonne Lincoln (1994) emphasize that qualitative

researchers are exploring ways to share stories, and Gloria Ladson-

Billings (1994) argues that stories have gained credibility as an

appropriate methodology for conveying the rich quality and

complexities of cultural and social phenomena.

In this study, parents' narratives contributed important ideas

that help us understand their experiences with the Individualized

Education Planning meetings in their child's school. Listening to the

experiences through their stories assisted in understanding their

perceptions, feelings, and other developments of their child's IEP

process. Emergent and salient themes, as well as punctuating words and patterns directed the organization of this study to assist the reader in comprehending the data collected. Indeed, an interactive link existed between the inquirer and the knower, whereby values are transparent.

Why Narrative Inquiry?

While there are several variations of the term "narrative," this study draws most heavily on Christine Bold's (2012) and D. Jean Clandinin's and F. Michael Connelly's (2000) delineation of narrative. According to Bold and to Clandinin and Connelly, narratives are situated around events, i.e., particular happenings within a certain time period or setting experienced by an individual. Narratives are the retelling of these particular events as that human experienced the event. These reflective accounts can carry a host of emotional sensibilities as they espouse a sense-making process (Bold, 2012). To Clandinin and Connelly (2000), narrative inquiry is a collaboration between the parties involved in a period of time, in place(s), and in a social interface with environments. It's simply a way of comprehending experience.

74

Narratives provide a wealth of information from the richness of experienced knowledge, while a survey does not have the capacity to convey such complex and situated information. Narratives are bound by human stories of experiences that address the indirect or direct complexities necessary to educate and learn (Webster and Mertova, 2007). It is humanly impossible to experience every experience experienced by every person in the world. However, narratives allow us to experience another's experience by bringing their sense of meaning of that experience into the narratives they relate. The aesthetics of storytelling provides a diversity of experiences simply in how it is told and provides a variety of ways it can be understood as varied as the number of people listening. Diversity in all senses of the word can connect via storytelling no matter who you are or where you are from.

There is no story without interaction of some sort. "Stories contain knowledge that is readily put to use in the world. In many instances stories do not simply contain knowledge; they are themselves the knowledge we want learners to possess" (Webster and Mertova, 2007 p. 20). Stories are naturally impregnated with restorative and engaging qualities. They have the impact to change lives of the storyteller and those listening (Bold, 2012). These reflective accounts carry a sense of therapeutic and emancipated relief (Sandelowski, 1991). "Narrative is not an objective reconstruction of life—it is a rendition of how life is perceived" (Webster and Mertova, 2007 p. 3). Debbie Pushor (2007) contends in her narrative inquiry that the stories of her parent participants juxtapose to those of teachers made for a multiplicity of stories that produced a wider spectrum of understanding from both sides. Narrative inquiry gave parents' knowledge a space otherwise usually not heard in a school setting (Clandinin et al., 2007).

Several disciplines including medicine and, especially, education are embracing the historic activity of storytelling. Scholars are relying on these narratives from those who are engaged with the events deviating from the traditional scientific ways of knowing (Banks, 1982). Traditional research methods, i.e., surveys and observations, have championed the retrieval of information for nominal studies that contend to capture parents' perspective of their experiences during the IEP process (Valle, 2011). However, these research methods do not always substantially lend themselves to determining how these parents negotiate their power within this space. The silence is so loud that the voices of the parents aren't heard. Some survey designs are restricted to a narrow response of the experience and the observer tells us what they observe of the experience. This is not to say these sort of strategies are wrong but they give no justice to the voice. Narratives are principal vessels that allow humans to construct meaning (Polkinghorne, 1988). Bold (2012) points out that contextual influence is situated in narrative inquiry making this research strategy standout from other methods. Valle (2011) claims she trusts narrative inquiry because of the human component. Narrative inquiry allows parents to respond in a more robust description of their personal lived experience:

> If we ask mothers to tell their stories, we learn about
> consequences of our practices within their lives. They
> have much to teach us about the impact of disability on

77

their identities as mothers and about the profound

experience of parenting a child with a learning

disability (pg. 188)

So, *Why Narrative Inquiry?* What we can learn from

parents' experiences through their narratives is

unmatched by surveys. There is a story behind that

"yes" there is a reason behind that "no." Clandinin et al.

place this question into perspective for all stakeholders.

METHODS

Parent Participants

The ten parent participants were recruited from three settings

using flyers, word of mouth, mass group email, and individual referrals.

The three settings were a local church bulletin, a local community

organization for families with children who live with special needs, and

a local children's medical center. Parent participants were selected from

a non-probability technique, purposive sampling. Purposive sampling is

applicable when participants share the same characteristics in knowledge

or experience about the research topic (McMillan and Wergin, 2010). To qualify for this study, parents had to have attended at least one IEP meeting and have a child who has been identified with multiple disabilities, also known as "concomitant impairments," under the disability category by the federal legislation. As much as I would have liked to hear all parents' experiences with their child's IEP process, it might have made for an equivocal study because parents' experiences with the IEP process could be quite different contingent on the child's disability. There were two benefits in restricting my study to a particular classification. First, it allowed my study to have more focus, which might lend itself to comparison of future studies, and second, my interestedness and lived experience is situated within this category.

Demographics of Parent Participants

The 10 parent participants range in age from 39 to 58 years old. Two of the 10 parent participants were married. Ethnic backgrounds included six Caucasians, three African Americans, and one native from India. Three parents earned high school diplomas with one having some college courses. Three parents earned associate's degrees. Three parents earned master's degrees, and one parent earned a doctoral degree.

79

Professions were as followed: systems logistics operator, security officer, registered nurse, secretary, adjunct college professor, physician, and educator. Two parents were stay-at-home mothers. Socio-economic status claims were one lower-middle class, eight middle-class, and one upper-class. There were two married couples that actually participated but there were four divorced participants and two married whose spouses could not participate. All parent participants' children were males with the exception of one parent who had a daughter. All parent participants were biological parents with the exception of one parent who was raising her nephew.

Interview Setting

Interviews were conducted in safe and conducive environments based upon the participants' request. The interviews occurred with or without spouses, depending on the comfort and availability of the parent, but if both parents participated in the interview, both must have attended at least one IEP meeting. Parents were given the freedom to tell their stories with minimal prompting and questioning during a one-on-one audiotape interview. One parent declined to be audiotaped.

Integrity of Recruitment

The parent participants were informed that the approval of Miami University and Institutional Review Board (IRB) was obtained prior to the implementation of the study. Participants completed an informed consent form. Participants were also cognizant of their right to continue or terminate their involvement with the study at any time with the assurance they would not experience any adverse reactions from their decision. The parents' identities will not be able to be identified through the dissertation or subsequent publications, leaving their identity to remain fully confidential.

Trustworthiness

Trustworthiness and confirmation of outcomes, data, and interpretation depend as much on the participants as the researcher. Trustworthiness was established through reflexivity and continuous verification of participants. Narrative inquiry recognizes that all measurements are fallible, and, therefore, multiple measures and observations are encouraged. Transferability (or comparability) is an internal validity that increases credibility to qualitative research. James

McMillan and Jon Wergin (2010) reiterate that qualitative study is what the study can teach us about other's lives. Stories are the heart of a qualitative study as they are entrenched with rich and thick descriptions to give better insight that one may find likeness in their environment. John W. Creswell (1998) and Clark Moustakas (1994) affirm that synergy of the researcher's perception and the knowledge acquired from the researched establishes inter-subjectivity. This back and forth motion creates social interaction which contributes to the making of solid verification. The reciprocal nature of inter-subjectivity makes for an in-depth understanding. Inter-subjectivity is an assessing value aiding in the validity of the study.

Moustakas posits, "establishing the truth of things" requires the researcher's perspective of the phenomenon to be taken into account (Moustakas, 1994, p.57). Reflection of one's own meaning of the experience and then that of those interviewed is needed to validate inter-subjectivity. The challenge of phenomenology is knowing how and in what way the personal experience of the inquirer is interjected (Creswell, 1998). Conversely, Allen Peshkin (1988) and Valle (2011) argue that subjectivity is inevitable and ought to be intentionally and methodically transparent in such work. Thus, there will be no question of ambiguity.

Transparent Subjectivity/Interestedness

It is imperative that I, as researcher, clarify my pre-understanding—my first-hand-personal experience within this body of work I present. Forthrightly, I have stated my personal experience throughout the first three chapters of this study. I live the experience as mother of a child who lives with multiple disabilities, is medically fragile, and has an IEP. I have lived the experience as an educator passionately engaged in the IEP process. I have served as an authority for my students in having to prove why I sought IEP intervention, as well as a Resource Advocate for those parents whose child had an IEP. The time invested in these roles certainly account for some trustworthiness and a wealth of experience as I have viewed the IEP process through the lens of each role—educator, parent advocate and mother. For me not to be transparent with my multiple layers of knowing to my reading audience and my parent participants would certainly give reason to question my trustworthiness. However, traditional qualitative research does not make it inviting for one to be subjectively transparent. Madeleine Leininger (1985) argues firmly that a researcher should not portray someone they are not. In other words, the researcher approaches the interview as themselves, then goes into an active role and denies their role as researcher. This could only produce untrustworthiness to the very people they are asking to be honest. This dishonesty may possibly destroy a potential relationship built on honest dialogue and trustworthy information.

What must be realized by all individuals is that we all have pre-understandings. We may not be aware of the instance we are engaged with gathering such insight until it is requested of us and then we reflect and realize that we were involved, but maybe too busy, during that particular situation to realize what we were experiencing (Ryan, 2011).

Transparency and Reflexivity

Transparency and reflexivity are two features that are concomitant to subjectiveness and interestedness in qualitative inquiry as the burden of responsibility falls heavily on the researcher who must be cognizant of what biases and assumptions they bring to the study. For this study, transparency is defined as being candid, open, or frank (Collins English Dictionary, 2013).

"Transparency requires not only a careful and detailed documentation of the entire process of inquiry for subjective use, but also a 'public transparency' that adds trustworthiness and persuasiveness to the work, and helps other inquirers, particularly novice researchers, to expand their horizons" (Hiles, 2008 p. 890).

Susan Smith (2009) asserts that reflexivity increases credibility and honesty because it totally embraces and reveals the subjectivity of the researcher. Jane Gilgun's (2010) explanation of reflexivity best depicts how it is utilized in this study:

"**Reflexivity** emphasizes the importance of **self-awareness, political/cultural consciousness** and ownership of one's perspective. Being reflexive involves **self-questioning** and **self-understanding**. To be reflexive is to undertake an **ongoing examination** of what I know and how I know it." (Gilgun, 2010, emphasis in original).

Being reflexive also encourages and allows one to have a shift in their understanding as information is collected and constantly interrogated (Jootun, 2009). According to Christina Bold (2012), participants' narratives can change depending on the following three aspects: 1.) temporal, 2.) meaning, and 3.) social as the researcher's responsibility to reflect and be reflexive can be transforming. "This can be useful, formative phenomenon, enabling revisiting, reviewing, and rethinking our ideas about the data, thus adding rigor to the research process" (Bold, 2012 p. 31). Reflexivity is a continuous practice of critical thinking. Helen Speziale and Dona

Carpenter (2007) advise the researcher to be clear of all their beliefs and assumptions before the onset of conducting the research. In a personal communication, Thomas Ryan, (December 5, 2012) agreed with Speziale and Carpenter's (2007) point and suggested that reflexivity should be an important technique for this study. Revealing the beliefs of the researchers encourages them to be candid and in tune to their own biases. This technique is an important part of what is traditionally known as bracketing or phenomenological reduction in phenomenological studies.

Journaling Through My Process

The researcher has a duty to demonstrate vigilant practices to overcome bias and prejudice (Schutz, 1994). For me, this included recording detailed personal and social interaction with my parent participants and personal journaling to challenge my own assumptions and root out bias. My journaling process took place at two different periods, i.e., before the evolution of my research and after my method was put into place but before interviewing parent participants. The process included the following steps: 1.) I wrote all I assumed and my own experiences about the IEP process before listening to narratives 2.) I took short memos during the actual interview process of my reactions and reflexive responses; 3.) I developed a transcript of the event by using the notion of reflection and developed a reflexive account that is made up of the notes I made and extended these notes to self; and 4.) I compared my two transcripts-reflective and reflexive (Ryan, personal communication December 5, 2012).

I have tried to make explicit the continuity in my experience—past, present and future and reveal how my experience may echo the participant's narratives in order to be fully transparent. According to Clandinin and Connolly, researchers "may note stories that occur as they 'work alongside' their participants, but more often they document doings, happenings, all of which are narrative expressions" (Clandinin & Connolly's, 2000 p.79).

Analysis of my Journaling Journey. One reason I believe parent participants felt comfortable in telling their stories to me was because they were not telling their story to an "objective researcher" but to another parent who they felt might better understand their experience. I am confident that if their stories were being told to another researcher at another time without the shared life experience, their stories would have been told differently. The different renditions depending on the position of the interviewer is inevitable. That my own position may bias their stories in one direction may be true, but no more true than the position of a different interviewer might bias the alternative rendition. As J. Elliot (2005) points out, narratives have three elements: temporal, meaningful, and social. Basically, these elements have the potential to demonstrate variations in the meaning of narratives depending on different time and social settings. Bold (2012) advises that we cannot expect a story told by one person to be told the same way in another setting. Thus, the contextual facet can define how the same story may be revealed differently. I take this notion a step further by applying researchers with like experiences. Bold (2012) argues that subjectivity in research isn't any less academic than a research that claims to be objective. She further purports that researchers depend on the experiences of those being interviewed and lack their own knowledge and experience. For me, my subjectivity increases my awareness and knowledge in my various roles as mother, educator, and researcher. John Mason (1994) insists that examination of self is essential in the research process; thus, higher education is guilty in not championing this notion.

I believe one quality in storytelling is the aesthetics in the varied narratives of similar scenarios. Stories are inextricable to the uniqueness of perspectives and are partial, so the ideal of varying narrative accounts from virtually the same experience creates a coopted complexity (Bruner, 2002). Butler-Kisber (2010) attributes mechanical thinking to positivist notions that we unconsciously believe in linear narrative. Before each interview, I practiced not to presume to know what their stories would reveal; I wanted to allow a space for all possibilities of experiences to be heard. Therefore, I approached each interview setting aside my own experiences. Advancing a personal agenda would have only defeated the purpose of this study that was to listen and understand what parents' narratives reveal about their experience of their child's IEP process. Reiterating

Valle's (2011) point, that parents', particularly mothers', narratives inform us of the effects of what is not working in educational practices in their lives. I suppose narratives will also inform us of the effects of what *is* working to continue to encourage productive and positive practices.

Experience is fluent and temporal as well as personal and social. I live the experience as mother of a child who lives with multiple disabilities, is medically fragile, and has an IEP. I have lived the experience as an educator passionately engaged in the IEP process. I have served as an authority for my students in having to prove why I sought IEP intervention as well as a resource advocate for those parents whose child had an IEP. The time invested in these roles certainly should account for some trustworthiness as I have viewed the IEP process through the lenses of each role.

Challenging Subjectivity

Paul Atkinson and David Silverman (1997) warn readers to be skeptical of personal narratives as they are not reliable. Such a warning questions the integrity of a researcher who enters into a study claiming to be objective by distancing themselves and claiming to be objective while also aiming to gain trust from the research participant (Leininger, 1985; Lipson, 1989 cited in Schutz, 1994). However, A.P. Bochner (2001) argues that personal narrative is rooted in navigating towards meaning, not seeking some objective truth. Narrative also allows those who may not otherwise have had the experience to be empathetic to others. It also allows for an awareness of a topic that carries the propensity to stimulate dialogue. Due to the process creating a sphere for challenging assumptions and critiquing practices, ultimately learning takes place. Butler-Kisber (2010 pg. 19) poignantly states, "In qualitative inquiry, no apologies are needed for identity, assumptions, and biases, just a rigorous accounting of them." Nonetheless, my interestedness as researcher carries the propensity to be challenged. In an article in the *Journal of Advanced Nursing,* Susan Schutz (1994) argues the following point: "An openly subjective approach allows the researcher to be a real partner with informants, and to openly use her own experiences and reflections in order to uncover valuable meaning and to find a different type of objectivity"

(p. 412). "To be challenged about your particular "subjectivity" is yet another example of the devaluing of mother knowledeges by the same power structures that you seek to critique. Irony at its best" (J. Valle, personal communication, March 9, 2012).

I, too, as Valle (2011, pg. 184) claims, believe my subjectivities will contribute to, rather than create a diversion from, the trustworthiness of this study. Subjectivity is actively functional throughout the research's entirety (Peshkin, 1988). If my subjectiveness/interestedness is challenged—my response is—"It's my wholeness; it's my completeness, it's the solidarity of all my identities that make me who I am".

CHAPTER 4: RESULTS

Introduction

In this chapter I share parents' experiences with their child's individualized educational program (IEP) discerned through their own narratives. I illustrate some of their stories metaphorically through categorized classical or popular stories, films, or aphorisms in hopes that the reader can understand the parents' narratives through a mutual place of knowing. A short summary is given of each classical or popular story, film, or aphorism as they were produced from the salient themes drawn from the parents' narratives. Next, an analogy of the parents' narratives is written to appreciate the juxtaposition to the classical or popular story, film, or aphorism. Finally, portions of the parents' actual narratives are analyzed, interpreted, and shared. The reader will find that several of the themes overlap as some excerpts could have been placed in two or three categories. Presented in this chapter are very different stories but similar experiences.

The purpose of this research was to listen and provide a missing voice in our understanding of the individualized education program (IEP) through the narratives of ten parents' experiences during their child's IEP. Thus, special education experts will understand through a parents' perspective how they might improve or in some instances affirm policies and practices. Narratives allow individuals to live vicariously through the voiced illustrations.

ONCE UPON...RESULTS

Alice in Wonderland

Summary

Alice in Wonderland is a classic storybook fable written by Lewis Carroll in 1865 that tells of a young girl situated in a land of mystic wonder with unfamiliar characters and dealings. She is overcome by directives and quandaries that, to say the least, are daunting. Fortunately, Alice's adventures are all but a dream as she emerges from her nap and life goes on as she knew it.

Analogy

Parents' initial experience during their child's individualized education program in special education in some cases is unfamiliar land. Like Alice, parents are confronted with directives reinforced by policies and procedures. However, these parents have a much higher stake—their child. Unlike Alice, this is the "new normal" for them. They do not wake up from a dream and live life as it was.

First IEP Meeting Experience

9.25.12 (couple). Wife: *I felt cornered... not knowing the laws. The process made us feel like we had to give into everything they wanted. Whatever **they** said... we thought.*

4.19.13(DW). DW: *It was very full, professionally supported. I felt really good and continued to feel this way. At first there was not a lot of parental direction in the development of the goals. It was largely coming from the educators.*

10.08.12 (AP). AP: *I was terrified because I didn't know what the heck it meant. At first it was difficult.*

11.11.13 (JK). JK: *I didn't know what to expect. I was really excited that a small school district was able to accommodate for a few kids with needs.*

2.25.13 (DG). DG: *The psychologist, teachers, and other people were involved. The IEPs have gotten harder because some of the teachers have been angry or disappointed with Josh because he's not doing what he is capable of doing. I haven't had the best experience with the psychologist. She's the first I experienced that seems not to have the interest of the child. She was more geared to what the teachers thought than what I thought or what was best for Josh. She was more concerned with what was best for the school than Josh. She would circumvent things; she heard myself and the other teacher agreeing to and bring it back to what was best for the school. It wasn't until a male teacher spoke up and said, "We may need to listen to the guardian because this may be the reason why we are in this predicament."*

10.5.12 (SD). SD: *I really didn't know what an IEP was. Mainly at that time it was about getting him to speak. It was a lot of people there. I really never had been happy with the IEP. I think they are kind of lame. I hate to say that but...I know they have to write things down and have to break things down but when I read them I'm like, "What a* *waste of time." "Like this right here...don't worry about this...it's no big deal." Let's try him functioning at home or him trying to do things for himself. Let's not focus on academics; it's like I'm trying to beat it into their heads and they're not listening. I do think I'm heard but they just don't know how to address my situation.*

7.11.13 (JH). JH: *(expressed laughter) It wasn't good. Well, first it was the Evaluation Team Report (ETR) and that really wasn't good. The psychologist had no idea who Matthew was and it basically ended with the special education supervisor telling me she wouldn't have the psychologist around us again. The psychologist did an IQ test on Matthew who was a little guy—3 years-old. Matthew was on my lap and the psych was showing him pictures asking Matthew to respond. I couldn't believe it...this was a waste of my time. I told him Matthew couldn't talk but he insisted this was the only way of testing him. That's how the testing went. Then the ETR meeting...I'm the kind of parent whose going to have every area assessed and then I'm going to read it all. I wrote all my questions that I wanted to ask. On their document there were misspellings, there were other people's names*

99

and information that wasn't even correct. I questioned where the psychologist got his results and he said he just guessed. He said he basically came up with the IQ number. I experienced how he assessed but I didn't know how he measured my son. The psychologist finally admitted he gave Matthew the lowest number he could. This was the kind of stuff going on at this meeting. The first meeting was very big and long because I had every person there that was supposed to be there. I was picking it apart because I thought it was my job to make sure this report reflected Matthew. I just remember me asking questions through the entire process. As a mom it was so easy for me to see stuff that wasn't true and didn't make sense. They didn't like it...they just wanted me to sign and be done.

Couples' IEP experience

9.25.12 (Couple 1). *Wife: I would be so angry when I left out those meetings because they would walk all over me.* **Husband:** *We told them they woke a lion; now you have both of our attention. I think being a woman the intimidation factor was there even though she's not the type that is easily intimidated.* **Wife:** *They made me feel like they* *knew better for my son. Example, (in sarcastic tone), "We are working on it...he will get there....we know what we are doing...we will continue working on it"* **Husband:** *Having both parents involved if at all possible makes a huge difference. Two parents present helps alleviate that ganged up feeling. We can play good cop/bad cop. I warm them up and she gets things on track.*

9.24.12 (Couple 2). *Wife: I've noticed that they may treat us better because we are*

together. They will literally congratulate us and say they are happy to see us both there.

Husband: They are surprised to see us there. ***Wife:*** *They're more surprised if we don't*

come in together now. ***Husband:*** *Actually, they will focus or gear more of the questions*

towards Mom because they are used to mothers coming in. We know they aren't trying to *be rude or have some sort of bias. **Wife:** Everything is always geared*

towards me.

The "New Normal"

Summary

This aphorism refers to the manner of which a person's usual way of knowing or dealing with a situation or life has been significantly altered. Therefore, it is a different way of doing something.

Analogy

The "new normal" to a parent raising a child who lives with special needs begins when their child is born. In some cases, the parent may not have a medical diagnosis of their child's disability. So, another dimension of "new normal" may set in when there is an acceptance of their child's condition as their lives will be affected from every domain. There will be positive and negative facets in the challenges that are surely attached to the "new normal". Every dimension of life such as simple daily living, personal lifestyle, relationships, finances, school, and health care will be affected.

Challenges

9.25.12 (Couple 1). *Wife: I think the most challenging was figuring out what was our son's diagnosis because he had so much going on. Every time we go to a doctor they would say he is a puzzle we may never figure it out. We were not satisfied with that answer.* **Husband:** *More testing got him to the point where he became self-aware…"what's wrong with me?"…"why am I different?" It became real challenging when he began comparing himself to others his age.*

4.19.13 (DW). **DW:** *Trying to get him to express his basic needs… "I'm hungry"… "I'm   thirsty."*

10.8.12 (AP). AP: *Hyperbaric oxygen treatment was an aggressive therapy. For six eeks he cried the entire time—JC is not a crier. Brain surgery was really challenging because they wanted him to have a seizure but he wouldn't. It was seven to 30 days long. Having to get acclimated to home again was challenging too.*

9.24.12 (Couple 2). **Wife:** *The winter is a challenge in trying to keep him healthy. Making the decision to keep him home or from school. If* *we have to take him out, then it's trying to get him back in because it's usually one or two weeks and then making sure he gets his medications. It takes him longer to get well and he has to take steroids…not simple medication for colds.*

4.19.13 (DW). DW: *My son performs very differently at home than how he does at school. I've had to record things my son does so they would believe me because they have questioned my statements that I've written in the communication log. There are numerous of things that has happened like this. That's why I think the biggest challenge for a parent with a child who has special needs is to educate others how that disability actually realistically impacts them as well as educate them on their prejudices and judgments made about people with disabilities. I often see with my son, professionals come to a conclusion but they don't question their bottom line or statement and they don't deconstruct. My son wanted to play basketball last year. It was written in his IEP. I had completed all the paperwork that was needed. However, the principal called and said they needed to discuss things and have a full IEP meeting so they could fully understand. This* *was a violation of Americans with Disability Act (ADA). I was the only parent having to prove fitness when the district was supposed to make accommodation for my son. They made the assumption because he was built a certain way that he couldn't play. They didn't question their own judgments about people with disabilities. They need to raise their expectations and judgments of my son and others with disabilities.*

7.11.13 (JH). JH: *Matthew has many medical diagnoses. The first time I heard of his struggles, I was 17 weeks into the pregnancy and I felt numb, lost, like I had no idea what a mom who has a child with such a diagnosis is supposed to do. I thought surely someone would tell me what to do, such as the doctors, but that was not the case. So I quickly learned that medicine is not exact and there is no prescribed way to move forward when a diagnosis is given. I learned that you have to trust your instincts and make decisions based upon the love you have for a child. Due to that love, you become the expert. I had to direct the medical people to give me the information I needed to make decisions. As we received more diagnoses, it was easier in regards to not feeling devastated as I did the first time. As more came, I gained* *the attitude that it is just another piece of the puzzle that we will understand and create a plan to get through daily living and meeting his distinct needs. I decided to go into special education after I learned about Matthew. I was scared because I didn't know what to do with him educationally. All I knew about special education was that it was a separate classroom students went to and it wasn't a regular classroom. I knew as a regular education Science teacher I had students on IEPs and the intervention specialist (IS) would come into my room with the student but she just sat in the back and didn't do a whole lot. So I was worried about Matthew going into a system like that.*

10.5.12 (SD). SD: *My son getting big is a challenge and getting him under control.*

7.11.13 (JH). JH: *I just got a new caregiver today. Yesterday the other caregiver came n and said Friday is her last day. I said, "Oh my Gosh you got to be kidding me." I had a busy day yesterday making calls to the agency. I told them I need to be at work in another city so they sent someone out today for me to meet and interview her. "I liked* *her, thank GOD...I didn't think I was." What are the chances of liking someone to care for your child the first meet? I interview all my caregivers. We are just getting Medicaid four years ago because they kept turning me down. I finally made it a priority; I was on my own and I needed to work. I couldn't work if I didn't have assistance before and after school. So it is a very big deal to let someone care for your medically fragile child. The agency and the caregivers just expect you to hire who they send out but it doesn't work that way for me.*

11.11.13 (JK). JK: *The challenge came with transitioning to a larger school district.*

7.11.13 (JH). JH: *A big challenge is trying to remember everything to do all the time. I feel like my mind is constantly going. Constantly preparing for what others are going to need to make the environment right for Matthew so whatever happens we got what we need. I do the same with hospitals. He just had a shunt revision in September and he had to stay in the hospital because of his asthma. So I'm monitoring his seizures and health and being ready to go so I can have all his meds and my bags packed. I'm thinking of all the times we've been in* *the hospital and we didn't have what we needed. His needs are so special and you think at a children's hospital that they should have all what he needs but they don't. If they do, you have to fight to get them or you have to wait and I'm not willing to do that and throw his schedule off. I just had a stay with the hospital that ended with me speaking with patient relations. I'm always trying to educate others so they can take better care of our kids.*

2.25.13 (DG). **DG**: *It's harder to remold another person's child.*

7.11.13 (JH). JH: *Trying to slow down and enjoy...we do. I've always been very adamant about Matthew being a part of the community that's my biggest thing for him as well. I want him to touch the grass, be at the ballgames, go the aquariums, and touch things. It has always been a challenge for him but as he gets older I see that that may not be what he wants. Just trying to gage when to push and when to back off can be a challenge. Another challenge is with him getting bigger. I have rotator cuff problems. I was at physical therapy tonight and I was told I had a mild tear. I don't want to do surgery because I will need six weeks to heal and I can't do that. Moving the wheelchair and* *moving him from one spot to another is getting really difficult and it's*

getting hard on me because I will have to figure out what to do.

The Gingerbread Boy

Summary

This classic tale from the May 1875, issue of *St. Nicholas Magazine* is about an elderly couple that longed for additional company. So, the elderly lady bakes a gingerbread boy who sprang from the oven and outruns both she and her husband. He continues to outrun everyone who sets out to catch him. Unfortunately, he finds his match with a sly fox and the gingerbread boy succumbs to his demise.

Analogy

Parents' having concerns of the individualized education program (IEP) being less than what the name implies was frequently voiced. In some narratives, the term "cookie cutter" was used. The comparison between The Gingerbread Boy and an IEP is not in the plot of the story but in the details that create each outcome. Hence, the irony is in the systemic manufacturing of each product. For instance, the traditional gingerbread boy cookie components are the eyes, mouth, arms, legs, and buttons for clothing. In comparison, the IEP components are the present levels of academic performance, annual goals; benchmarks or short-term goals, measuring and reporting progress, special education and related services, supplementary aids, and program modifications or individual accommodations. Depending on the age and grade of the student, the IEP may contain additional content. The details of the creation of the gingerbread boy and an IEP are essential in the function of each product. However, the lack of individuality for a gingerbread cookie is much more acceptable than the lack of it in an IEP. From a parents' perspective, individuality is what is significant in the value for their child's success. Hence, the "cookie cutter" model should not be valid in the IEP process.

9.25.12 (Couple 1). *Wife (mocking teacher): "Oh we've had a child with Asperger's before; we've had a child with Obsessive Compulsive Disorder (OCD) before" but you haven't had **my** child. **Husband:** There are good intentions behind the IEP and the No Child Left Behind (NCLB) assessment testing is rooted in good ideas. **Wife**: But every child is not a "cookie cutter" same child. **Husband:** The* *integrated classroom fails because they don't have plans to teach*

those kids who need extra.

10.08.12 (AP). AP: *I will say that all the IEPs have been the same.*

Even though they ay they are not the same, they are... it's the same

criteria. They say that IEPs are supposed to individualize the child but

they don't. They got this thing that this is all we have to do. This is

what the state provides or require. For example, JC can't read but he

knows certain emblems. Gear a curriculum aimed towards the things

he can do. Those are the things that I don't care about IEPs. So they

say, "This is what we should be working on for a 14 year-old with

Cerebral Palsy (CP)." He's not going to ever read or take a pin and

write by himself. They try different programs on the iPad but I had to

take my own money and purchase the program and JC likes that.

That's not where the school system is right now. If I could change

anything about the system, it would be just because my son has CP

doesn't mean he's like other children with CP. I think there are some

people in the system that listen but there are some who will not "think

out the box"—they will refer to a text book to make every child fit

... "But it says right here, a 14 year-old with CP should be working on this and it works." Well, no it doesn't. You get those school professionals who are strictly by the book who do not want to step out of those areas. Unfortunately, those who make the final decision are not the aides who work with my son. You can suggest, but they won't step out the box.

10.5.12(SD). **SD:** *The main issue is that they got my son in this real small room in a small area with other kids that are loud too. It's like they are bouncing off one another and the noise level is out of control. So, now you want an autistic kid to concentrate on his and do all this while all this stuff is going on...it's not going to happen. I've walked in there myself and said this is like hell for my kid and he's supposed to behave and act appropriately. They have that one room and they can't do anything about it...that's it. They have all these kids feeding off one another with the noise and some are sound sensitive and there's hollering and screaming. I don't have the answers to this. I look to them...they have all the degrees. The only thing I can think of is, if he had a tutor, one-on-one, and not be in that room at all. I've suggested*

112

that, but they can't do it. They are short of staff down to 1.5 and more

kids who are autistic and medically fragile. The only thing I'm looking

forward to is him getting out so he can use his creativity. At this point,

they are just trying to keep themselves and others from getting injured.

Every autistic kid is so different. It's hard to train someone about them

because they are all so different. They can be like night and day. What

works on this kid may not work on another kid. My son is really a

great kid. He smiles and likes to have fun. It's so sad that he is

miserable at school and the teachers are probably miserable too.

7.11.13 (JH). JH: *There is a difference between private and public*

schools. Public I feel like a number and the big joke is they know me...

they know I'm going to question them. Why don't they come in with

their "A" game? It's like they don't care. All the goals are the same.

It's like they take another kids IEP and put Matthews name on it. Now

that I write IEPs, it has made me more tolerant. I understand they are

overworked. I know they have all these laws. It's made me a better

Intervention Specialist, but it's not so overwhelming that I cannot

individualize every IEP for my families. Public school is so "cookie

113

cutter". My big thing during his first ETR when he was three-years old was that they wanted to start him off in a classroom with one teacher and three aides. There was no reason why he couldn't have been in the least restrictive environment and see if he have challenges then move him. They didn't want to give him a chance. He would never get out into a regular classroom because the special education teacher does not want to lose those aids. He couldn't even get a one- on- one aide at the public school. I don't nderstand what constitutes an aide. If you leave him in the same spot in the morning he will be there in the same spot in the afternoon soak and wet because he can't do anything for himself. So that's why they said he should be in a special education classroom with the teacher and the aides. Then, I feel they are restricting him because he's not in the regular classroom. They felt he would make noise and distract the other students. If he's in a regular classroom the students will get use to him. You can go into classrooms and there are always kids talking and they are doing things. Private school they never had a child like Matthew so they pretty much did things like I asked but that came with raising money to get things like

114

an elevator and in-services to train for inclusion. I have been able to prescribe and work closely with these teachers. In the beginning they were mortified. I knew I could tell them a million things, but I let them have Matthew for a week and ask them to write questions after experiencing him. They learned by experiencing him. By the end of the year, they were all so happy and grateful for the difference Matthew had made for them and to see the students and the others families grow because of him. My experience at the private school is quite different than the public school. He's never had a teacher that didn't do well with him...it has been all good. It's been a very rich experience. I feel supported at the IEP meetings. I feel listened to, although I still have to direct a lot but they also don't have a lot as well. I've learned to balance Occupational Therapy and Physical Therapy (OT/PT) (occupational and physical therapy) services. Private school provided an one-on -one aide for him.

Groundhog Day

Summary

Groundhog Day is a 1993, American comedy starring Bill Murray who plays an arrogant and narcissistic television weatherman who is forced to re-evaluate his life and ethical center after covering a Groundhog Day event. He continues to relive the same detailed actions every morning he awakens. What's further disturbing and perplexing is that those around him appear to be moving about their day in a mechanical and mundane manner. He seems to be trapped in a never ending timeless loop.

Analogy

Groundhog Day was the way a parent in my interview piloting process expressed her frustration with the IEP. I thought it was a brilliant expression in how she made meaning of the sometimes repetitive mechanical actions of the staff and special education system

9.25.12 (Couple 1). *Wife: Teachers not reading an IEP is very frustrating. Husband: They go into the year not knowing their students in their classroom. Wife: Or, they think they know them because they*

116

read the diagnosis but didn't read it thoroughly. **Wife:** *We made a list of all things that set our son off and what can help him. We explained this before the school year and this seem to help.* **Husband:** *But the teachers we met with at the end of the year were not the ones we met with earlier in the year. So, it was like starting all back over again. In the meeting, the teachers responsible for his curriculum were one was doodling, one looking at her phone, and the other teacher sitting in the back...I'm not sure if he even absorbed anything. So the work sent home by these teachers was even questioned by the home instruction teacher who fortunately knew our son from the previous year. They obviously didn't read the IEP and didn't know him because the work was not attainable for him. Had they taken the time to read the IEP and listened during the meeting we wouldn't have had the growing pains we went through as we did last year. It's like we do it over each year.*

10.8.12 (AP). AP: *Almost all the time the IEP is already written up. I had to stop them because they would have the same things all the time, like working on his writing but it was making him upset. To make him* *hold a pencil and write something...it's not going to happen. I finally*

had to say I think your time will be much better spent offering things

he knows already. That's when they borrowed an iPad, but when I was

talking about purchasing an iPad they were like, "Whoa...wait a

minute" ... they start talking about all the things they have to do to get

it and all the people that are involved. Then the idea it's put off to next

year. That's why I go off and do things on my own.

10.8.12 (AP). AP: *They will send a paper home before the IEP to ask*

you for your ideas but when you get to the meeting you realize that it is

the same paper you got last year; they are just changing the date. I do

realize their hands are tied. It's like your child has CP—your child has

autism so this is what we do. These papers are formed; it's like

checking off something that is done. The dates are just changed... like

placing an order for equipment and you use the same form every

month but change the dates. We are talking about our kids not

equipment.

10.5.12(SD). SD: *The purpose of the IEP for my son has been limited.*

You can see this on the IEP. They want him to do this and that three times a day but he rarely makes those goals. I know they have to have it for documentation but he has had some goals for years. We've discussed food to get him to do things and now they are having to use food just to keep him under control. He's gained 10 lbs. in two months. The IEP has not changed a lot and he has the same goals year after year. Now, they can't address all of the goals because of the behavior and noise.

9.24.13 (Couple 2). *Wife: It seems like the teacher puts goals on the IEP that they need for that grade level but they don't necessarily work on it. So you come back for another IEP and its still on there but it's not a focus. They can have things on IEP for three or four years. I would like to see them work on it and make note that they have worked on it and mastered it and then see how they are addressing it if they are not progressing.*

Aha Moment

Summary

An "aha moment" is an aphorism that refers to the enlightenment, realization, and understanding of something. It is an awakening of a consciousness during a meaningful situation.

Analogy

The journey of living a life as a parent of a child living with special needs is a continuous learning trajectory. In some cases the "aha moment" begins in the acceptance of their "new normal".

Particular meaningful moments *(positive and negative lessons learned or an awakened consciousness)*

9.25.12 (Couple 1). *Husband: "Never give up"...Wife "You can't change things; take a positive from a negative situation and learn from it". Husband: "You're only given what you can handle and when you think you've had enough (chuckle) it's more to come."*

10.8.12 (AP). *AP: I've learned that the little things are important.*

4.19.13 (DW). **DW:** *To see value in progress and shifts in my son's behavior, cognition, and his emotional growth. For someone who teaches and has a child with these disabilities just to seize it, value it, be thankful and grateful for that progress he's made, however small it is.*

10.8.12 (AP). **AP:** *Being a parent of a child with special needs, you just want your child to be considered as normal as anyone else. Can he go and run around like everyone else? Maybe not, but if you put him in his walker, he's going to try to do what he can do. Sometimes the ideas you come up with may be hard because you may have to do a little more work with them.*

10.8.12 (AP). **AP:** *There was a time when my son was having trouble in school and he was pulling pages out of the books. I don't take up for my son because I know what he can do but I also know he had to be aggravated to be accused of something as such. So I visited the school without notice and watched him maneuvering himself around on the floor pulling things off the shelves trying to get the attention of the person responsible for watching his class. She did not redirect him to* *do something else. I was livid! He was off by himself doing whatever. He wanted her attention. If I hadn't seen it for myself, the school officials was going to write him up. They think because some individuals with disabilities don't talk or they don't walk they don't know anything. That's something very upsetting because you trust people with your child.*

9.25.12 (Couple 1). *Husband: After third grade, we begin learning the laws and stopped depending on them to tell us everything. We began to take more control of our son's education and became informed parents and advocates as opposed to our son being pushed around in the system. **Wife:** We kept seeing the gap and then there was the incident with the scissors. Again, we weren't aware of the laws so we're given this book, **Whose IDEA is This**. To decipher the book isn't really easy. **Husband**: The book doesn't cover a lot of the law, the book covers what they want you to know—the minimum. It's when you get into the law of special education what the schools are required to teach; required modification; least restricted environment is when we really start to learn our rights. **Wife:** Talking with other parents*

122

and speaking with an advocate who sent lots of formation on how to write an IEP. **Husband:** *Really up until the third grade they would basically bring in the IEP document to meeting and act like… here it is. They would go through it and we would sign it.* **Wife:** *They weren't altering his work for his level. They were basically given him the work but just cutting the amount. They were given him eighth- grade reading questions and he was on a fourth- grade reading level. There were no accommodations and he didn't understand.* **Wife:** *They made goals so high it was unattainable or goals so easy that he easily made them. We've seen less of this practice since the seventh and eighth grade because we are more aware. You must choose your words wisely. I think sometimes the schools practice this way to benefit themselves the less work they have to do.* **Husband:** *It also revolves around money… they provide a minimum amount for certain services and find a loop hole to use for something else. They are educated professionals so they know what they're doing. When they come across parents who are equally as informed it takes them by surprise.*

9.25.12 (Couple 1). Husband: *The positive of how the IEP has been on our son is we been able to focus on needs opposed to just letting him get pushed along with receiving just enough. Seventh- grade is the first time our son is now reading from billboard signs! We are actually seeing increased reading level, recall, and retention week to week. His anxiety level has improved just and overall absorption of material. He's buying books on his own. Our communication has improved with the school. I think they realize that they are going to hear us every week or every couple of days until things get smoothed out. If something is good we let them know when things are working.*

4.19.13 (DW). DW: *Particularly in the last few years, I have had some serious concerns with the materials, methods, adaptations, and curriculum development. So I have had significant lengthy IEP processes because it took a long time to get the goals developed. In my move to Ohio, I took a much more active role in the IEP. The IEP seem, to me, to be ineffective, poorly researched, and unorganized-- not comprehensive. Consistently, the teachers did little research on methods and materials to play to my son's strengths and to build up* *his weaknesses in the classroom. The most difficult awareness I've learned is with all the participants and their advanced degrees in these rooms and all they seem to be more focused on, collectively, is coming up with how many minutes a month they can offer for therapy. It's challenging to get them to see my child's needs and what needs to happen to facilitate movement forward and productive functional action on their part so it can be a shift for my son. From their perspective I am a difficult parent, intimidating, threatening, too assertive, and too nitpicking. I have to keep my focus on my child and make sure they come to the table with the same intention. They often do not have integrative comprehensive views together. So that if the OT or PT isn't aware that the speech therapist (ST) and intervention specialist (IS) are working on vocabulary or common language, it presents a significant conflict for the child. Lately, it has helped that the ST is aligned with my perspective. It has helped tremendously and assisted my son in communication, socialization, and other skills he needs.*

4.19.13 (DW). DW: *One thing I did was ask at the beginning of the IEP if each person*

could tell from their perspective how my son has changed over that year. It was a good

experience for me because I think it made them all think in a different way. Several

people told me later that every IEP meeting should start that way. After IEP meetings, I

generally feel I'm glad it's over with, but not often sure there is a sense of urgency or

importance in ensuring that this is implemented accurately, effectively, or contractly. Trying to remember what's important... it's not about me or my ego it's my son. It's been just so frustrating.

9.24.12 (Couple 2). Wife: *Even at the IEP, the teacher had negative things to say. It's like she made things bigger than what they were. Her issues and concerns were not valid. Example: he doesn't play with* *the bad kids and he doesn't talk in class but he's very loud on the playground. The other professionals didn't agree that these were issues of concerns. My husband and I were happy that they saw what we had been going through.*

10.8.12 (AP). AP: *You have good experiences and then you have to move on to the next level and it might not be the same. My son had a communicator device attached to his chair to assist him; it would go wherever he would go and everyone including me was going to have to learn how to use it. The teacher did not want this in her class because this would be an interruption and yet another child in a wheelchair. This was a known thing with this teacher to not be cooperative. Although JC was potty trained he would have accidents off and on. I noticed him coming home with mess still on his butt. Then the special education supervisor calls me and ask how would I like to start putting JC in pampers again because the aides were having trouble with this. I said, "Absolutely not." He's worked too hard to get to this point. You will have to watch for his sign pointing down and take him to the restroom. I bought gloves for all the aides and what it came down to* *was the aides didn't feel comfortable with touching his penis. I*

constantly got letters stating how combative he was and how stressful

it was to get his pants over his braces and it was just too much. One

time I had surgery and the school knew this. I got a call after my third

day of surgery asking me to pick him up because they refuse to change

his pants because he was combative. I was told he was sitting in the

hall with poop in his pants. I was told he offended one of the aides and

he was suspended for the day. I appealed the suspension and lost. I

discreetly received a call from another educator who told me I might

want to push this further for a state investigation. When they came to

investigate, this particular teacher tells the state "this is who I am",

"this is my teaching", "I do not give care for these kids", "I do not

potty these kids", "if they're not here to learn they don't need to be in

my classroom"...she is still teaching. Our representative made this

point: "How would you feel if someone wanted you to wear pull-ups

and you knew how to use the restroom but people are talking about

you and not wanting to change you?" They granted me to move to

another school. The next year in third grade the reputation followed that I was one of those moms and he was a combative child. I knew

this would happen—that this reputation would follow us. I was told

that if you weren't nice to me I would call my attorney. I knew people

where feeling this way I could just feel the tension. Sometimes you can

feel so alone because you have these professionals sitting around you

and judging you and you feel like the "Lone Ranger".

2.25.13 (DG). DG: *The psychologist walked into the IEP and*

acknowledged everyone around the table but me. She didn't even

speak to Josh. She was not child-friendly or people-friendly; it was just

associate-friendly. Most of the time, before she was a part of the

meetings, I felt like I have been a participant in the meetings and I

have been heard. I interject anyway, even if I feel I am not being

heard. They have had pre-written IEPs, but they will mail it before we

meet. Some of the people do listen to what I say because the social

worker will ask how everyone feel about my suggestions and ask the

teachers, does it fit into the classwork. The teachers would agree. The

parents should be more inclusively involved in the planning, not just

signing off at the end. They should be pre-engaged.

9.24.12 (couple 2). Wife: *I've learned to be patient. He's much more independent because I'm used to doing for my other son who has CP. He's also taught me to allow my other son, with CP, to do things on his own because he is stronger and older now.*

10.5.12(SD). SD: *His one teacher is good. She understands that I just want him to gain the skills to do things on his own around the house, but she says they don't have those things available in the district. I try to use the things they want me to use at home but it is not practical at home because I will never get things done. They're trying to encourage talking but they are having so much trouble with his behavior now. His behavior has always fluctuated. My son has so much going on and they have other kids to deal with. Earlier in his schooling I think the teachers knew what to do with him.*

9.24.12 (couple 2). Wife: *We feel like we are participants within the IEP. Our IEPs are pre-written but they ask us about things. I think the first teacher was a little over zealous and made things bigger than what they were; this teacher is more in tuned to him. She rewards him more and we talk often. We think the IEP has supported our son.*

130

10.5.12(SD). SD: *Lately they have been writing the IEPs and send them home for me to look at it before we meet. If I have issues, I will call and see if it could be changed. If they don't make the changes, I will reiterate what I asked them do. I've told them I rather they focus less on academics because all it's doing is frustrating him. He's smart... I know he can learn things but he's getting older and he needs more on transitioning; he's almost an adult.*

9.24.12 (couple 2). Wife: *It was the way the teacher came at us like something was seriously wrong with him—blaming game. Complaining he doesn't know anything but he knew these things because he could do them at home. There was even an argument in front of him that shouldn't have happened. The teacher said she thought it was selective mutism but all along it was his medication that needed to be changed. None of the experts agreed that it was selective mutism because of his other interactions they observed him doing.*

10.5.12(SD). SD: *The teachers are having a difficult time just trying to keep their selves from getting choked by my son. These are tiny little ladies trying to control him. Sometimes I have to physically hold him.*

He's been doing better in the last week because I told them if they get him more physically active it will keep him occupied. They also have been putting weights on his legs occasionally. This was suggested by the OT.

7.11.13(JH). JH: *I had to learn to let others help. I wanted to do it all. We have had therapy since he was one year—old and I had people in and out my house all the time. We had good ones but they go and move on so you learn to appreciate them and don't take them for granted because they probably have to move on soon. I've learned not to take things for granted. When Matthew was born I was told he has to work hard to see; he has to work hard to hear—it just don't come natural. His brain isn't working the way that it should. I remember thinking, "Gosh everything he does, everything that we do that is a reflex or natural but he has to work at it."*

10.5.12 (SD). SD: *I've learned to find the humor in things.*

7.11.13(JH). JH: *I've also learned diversity, whether it's religious, race, disabilities, or social economic but really embracing and* *pushing those around to embrace as well. I've learned difference is good—really to know yourself and what are your challenges. This has helped me with my students in pressing upon them that they have to know their disability and what does it mean and what can you do with it. Having Matthew has made me a better teacher. I've had kids with learning disabilities and hadn't given it a thought as to what I needed to do different with them.*

11.11.13 (JK). JK: *Be reasonable. I learned its best to be quiet and let them talk during the IEP meetings. "They know more about what to do with your child than you if you don't have the experience." Small districts are more accommodating and larger districts are not as sensitive to accommodating. My request for my child to get off the bus first was refused. My child had a seizure before the school district's transportation department accommodated my request.*

7.11.13(JH). JH: *I went into special education wanting everything for Matthew and once I learned that that wasn't going to happen, I went through due process. I went talking with the special education supervisor and superintendent. I looked at the future and saw what it*

133

was going to be. I looked at what Matthew had and saw the information I had brought to the attention of these people and decided at that point that I had done as much as I'm going to do at this point. My decision was let me put him in the system and see how things go. If it's hurting or not allowing him to progress in any way, then I will come back and address it. Another big lesson is I try to listen to my intuition and don't doubt it. When it says something is wrong, I will go back to the drawing board and make changes.

10.8.12 (AP). **AP:** *I've learned to pick my battles. Because if you complain about everything then you become one of those moms and then they won't listen to you at all. I've learned to let certain things go if other things are working. I do feel IEPs are necessary but what are they for if they are not individualized. My son can call out every letter with the game "Will A Fortune". How come they can't do something that allows him to show what he knows? It's not like I think they don't care or they don't see what I see but it's like this is what we do and this is what we are going to do. I don't blame the teachers and aides.*

7.11.13 (JH). JH: *The whole team aspect is positive. At the private school, I enjoy sitting in a meeting with OT and PT experts. I trust and listening to them tell me this is what we need to do. It takes the burden off of me. Typically the OT and PT experts ask the parent what they want. That's great. I'm going to tell you want I want and then I want you to tell me how this can happen because you have the knowledge, education, and experience—I don't. But I've learned over the years, I have to. I should have my medical degree by now. I'm telling doctors and nurses what to do because they don't know how to care for him and they should be telling me. I like to be able to relax and hear what experts have to contribute.*

4.19.13 (DW). DW: *I think the IEP helps in transitioning, focus, and provides some since of clarity to those working with him regarding his needs.*

9.25.12 (couple I). Wife: *I have seen a lot of couples who have children with disabilities or IEPs and it either brings you together in a relationship or pulls you apart. It was a time that we were angry and blamed each other but it was the schools fault. That's when the*

135

transition happened; instead of fighting one another, we became a team.

7.11.13(JH). JH: *I looked at him and said, "I can either break or make this child," because he is going to depend 100% and I have to do the best that I can. My strength came the day I found out he was going to have problems. The doctors sent us to genetic counseling and my world was changed. I didn't know what I was going to write, what I would ask. I don't know what they're going to be talking about. But it took me to keep telling my story to others and consoling them while I was consoling myself as well that I understood things a little better.*

4.19.13 (DW). DW: *One time I had an experience with my son when we were on a ferry in New York City. He was staring out the window and I was just at a loss that day of all he could not do. I was thinking, I wish I could teach him about dinosaurs or I wish I could talk to him about math. I was so sad. I just sat there feeling that way. Then I heard a kids voice say, "Mom, what are we going to do today. Are we going to go to the museum?" I was sitting there saying, I wish my son could talk to me like that. The ferry docked and we stood up and I turn* *around to see this little boy and he's in a wheelchair—his legs did not work. I just went okay, I got it, I got it. That to me was a very clear moment that I needed to get on with it. "This is what you have...this is what you have." That story is so vivid and in some ways I feel uncomfortable sharing it because it's like me comparing this to that. For people who have children with physical disabilities, it sounds like I'm slighting them but I'm not. I had this recognition and it was a very profound lesson for me. It was a **big aha!***

Accountability, Power and Rights...Oh My!

Summary

This aphorism was taken from the classical chant in "The Wizard of Oz" when Dorothy, Scarecrow, and Tinman were walking through the frightening forest—"Lions and Tigers and Bears...Oh My!" Naturally, they were fearful of the unknown of the possibilities within the wicked forest.

Analogy

The likeness is in the unspoken imagined fear behind the words—accountability, power, and rights. The phrase "Oh my" tends to heighten the possibilities. All three words can be imagined in the lives of parents introduced to special education. However, there are parents who never had to deal with these terms from an academic perspective until they entered the forest of special education. The efficacy of these words will be realized from the parents' narrative response.

4.19.13 (DW). DW: *Although I feel like an active individual, I don't believe there's anything about the process that makes parents equal. The IEP aims to make parents involved but not really engaged, not really equal. As a participant, they ask for your feedback; they want to hear it, but it isn't really weighed.*

9.24.12 (Couple 2). *Husband:* I wish they would listen to us more. We do know our kids. It's not like we are trying to go against them and what they do. They just need to recognize that we are experts too.

10.5.12 (SD). *SD:* I try to be flexible with the teacher because I know what kind of hell they go through in that classroom. I don't mean to discount those who are higher up but they really don't have a clue

what is going on at that level. I've had trouble with the school

medicating my son. The teachers want the medication given at one

time and I want it given at another time. You can't give medication too

close in hours. I don't appreciate teachers telling me how to medicate

my son. Teachers are not nurses. It's frustrating. It's just too many

people involved. I almost feel like the team is too big. I wish it was just

me and the teacher—she's the one who has come up with some of the

best ideas. I think it's a bad idea to have kids with autism all in the

same classroom together. They set each other off and the noise level is

something that isn't good with the sensory issues. I really don't have

the answer; that's why I keep looking to the people with the

experience.

7.11.13(JH). *JH: The same guy that did Matthew's IQ testing was at*

another ETR meeting when Matthew was in the fourth grade in public

school. It was worse than the first experience I had with him earlier.

Again, he was inconsistent making horrible statements. I would

question his results and his response, again, was he made it up. He

even said something like, "Come on, let's face it. Matthew can't do a lot." It got real uncomfortable for the people in the room because I called him out.

9.25.12 (Couple 1). Husband: *It was a fight to have the teacher to take the homework and make it multiple choice or fill-in. We just wanted it to be standard.* **Wife:** *We were told that's not how Ohio Achievement Assessment (OAA) works. They were worried about the OAA test. We aren't here for the OAA. We are here for our son's education, or him continuing growing and succeeding and gaining milestones, instead of sweeping things under the rug. We want him to do the work at his level and with modifications.* **Husband:** *By the way, the entire time our son is making straight "A's" and on the Honor Roll. So that brings in the question of whether they are really looking out for NCLB or is it just lip service they're pushing him along, so he's not left behind, and giving him the grade to keep him going along. That's when we said, "No" this isn't going to happen anymore. The work he does is going to be graded on what he does and not what the teacher helped him do. After fighting for that, it was clearer how far he really was behind in reading.*

4.19.13 (DW). *DW: I would keep asking the teacher to send information about the curriculum and modified schedule but I never got anything. So, I write to the supervisor of special education. She would be like okay. Nothing would happen. So, I go to the principal eventually; three-quarters into the process they become compliant. Who coordinates the implementation of IEPs? This is a problem. There's no one there making sure the implementation is taking place. Unless the parents push back, it's figured that this is what is happening. So I keep my own records. The relationship I had with the teacher, principal, and supervisor of special education were all bad because I was questioning and pushing back. I thought they could care less what I thought. After someone outside of the district came to observe the teaching in the classroom, it was accepted that things needed to be changed. They wouldn't listen to me, though, it had to come from outside. They know my background as an educator. Now my son has been doing so much better. I'm a good scholar. Thank GOD I know how to research because I look into everything. Our relationship isn't collegiate at all. They could have asked me if there*

141

were approaches to resources they could considered, but they didn't

do that. When they gave me the IEP document, I would come back with

a list of questions. I made a matrix of my questions, points, and legal

issues that are contentious that aren't being addressed or approaches

that they're not using. I am not afraid of them. I am very aware of my

position as an educated individual. I think of other parents who don't

have what I have and question things. Most parents don't question the

IEPs, they just sign it.

2.25.13 (DG). DG: *I used to feel apprehensive not knowing what they*

were going to do or say. So I used to just sign the paper, but then I

figured this doesn't make sense. This changed when they suggested

something that I thought wasn't right. So, I called a meeting. I used to

feel I was basically there to sign papers.

9.25.12 (Couple 1). *Husband: We have been fortunate for my wife to*

be at home, which is a full- time job, researching, and gathering

information while our son is doing homework. You hear these great

terms like NCLB and parents think the school is going to take care of

their child. No, they are not. It's the parents' responsibility. **Wife:**

They will do the least minimum. **Husband:** *They will get by through the minimum level of the law. Then, when you have become informed and involved you can get them to do it. As long as they think they have you where they can just get by.* **Wife:** *We are at the point now that we can walk into the Superintendent's office and ask to talk with them. It has been a fight but we wouldn't have had such a good relationship if we had taken things to court. There has been so many times we were told to get a lawyer for incidents. The school was going to pay for him to go to another school and offered other options but we opted not to because it's the school's responsibility.* **Husband:** *You don't have to resort to being mean. This leads to open lines of communication. By doing things in a civil way we have had more things done for him. It started off either way, though. We have been close to due process and have been told to do so. We have had people from the district very upset because we have been steadfast.*

4.19.13(DW). *DW: The teachers, intervention specialist, or supervisor of special education ask that the principal be present because I was too nitpicking, direct, or assertive. I have had a lot of* *this kind of experience. I say, "thank you," and go on to the next appointment. It's not about my personality. What I see is the school system trying to shift the power relationship constantly to put me in a lower position than them. It always has been in terms of my sense of maintaining that egalitarian approach. From my perspective, a sense that if I were more humble and be nice to everybody things would be okay. What I take from this is that you want me in a position that I don't question you. So, you are holding something over me and the power relationship is disparate. That awareness is difficult and negative. One day I sent an email to the principal and he tells me he understands that I didn't sign-in to **his** school. I responded, "I thought it was **our** school". This sort of stuff reminds me of a book called "I'm okay, You're okay". Transactional analysis is the different roles people take and the role they choose to come back and respond. For instance, if someone talks to you from a parent role but talks to you like a child, how do you come back as a parent, child, or another role? That's what I see with them. I don't know if they are so entrenched in their "teachery role" that they can't see that they don't need to talk*

144

that way to everybody. I refuse to be talked down to. It's been very

difficult for me in Ohio.

11.11.13 (JK). **JK:** *Attitudes were more or less, if we accommodate*

for one, we have to do for all. I had a problem with a person making

decision who knows nothing about my child. You tell them what you

want and how does it fit into their rules.

2.25.13 (DG). **DG:** *I don't think her issue with me has anything to do*

with being a

parent. I think it has to do with me being black and living in a

suburban area. From my experience, the psychologist attitude is like

*"**We** know what **we** are talking about" and I'm just to sit here and let*

them handle it. I never expressed this or addressed it because it is not

impeding on Josh's progress. Sometimes you can feel like the IEP is

like a "battleground". One time we were in a meeting and both

teachers were getting after Josh and he has an anger issue. I told them

he can only listen to one of them at a time and the parenting belongs to me. They're not going to badger him. I wasn't argumentative but I was firm.

9.25.12 (Couple 1). **Husband:** *Something happened over the summer because before the end of last year Home Instruction was, according to the school, temporary for him in the first semester. Then we have the first IEP for the year and they changed Home Instruction to the first half of the year with possibility of extending the entire year. Our first thoughts were funding and how is this benefitting the school district? Public school districts want to do what benefits them financially. They really pushed to get him changed over to autism. It was coerced. We agreed because we talked to his developmental specialist. We know it all revolves around money.* **Wife:** *Schools get more money for students with autism. We done hours of research seeking resources like Ohio Center of Autism and Low Incidence (OCALIO) and Ohio Coalition for the Education of Children with Disabilities (OCECD). A lot of people don't know it's out there.* **Husband:** *The schools don't tell you.* **Wife:** *Our IEPs have gone from six to10 pages and 30 minute meetings to half-inch thick IEPs.*

146

Husband: We now have three to four meetings before an IEP is finalized. We go in, get a draft. They come back after making the changes and we review the IEP. *Wife:* They have tried to alter numbers in working with him for certain amount of hours in areas. They have tried to take the aide services out. *Husband:* We look at it and say this is not what we agreed on. So, they have to go back and make a change. We go through a lot of meetings to set this up. A lot of parents don't know that. The schools say, "Okay, see you next November," and parents don't realize there is so much more they can be doing.

10.5.12 (SD). *SD:* They asked me what do I suggest and I said a bigger classroom but that's not going to happen. The teachers would like better things too but they're running up against brick walls too.

9.24.12 (couple 2). *Wife:* His teacher took it upon herself to change his schools, against our wishes, because she thought it would be better for him to be in a full day classroom. He never made a connection with her and we don't know if it's because he knew we were arguing back and forth with her. She made us feel that we should have kept him *where she put him because he was having trouble in her class. The things she complained about were not valid. I thought it might be something else like the medication he was on. It was the medication that was making him behave differently. We had to bring documentation showing that he should not be tested while on these medications. After the medication episode, he became a different kid.*

7.11.13(JH). *JH: I went into these meetings with the ideas that I know this process. I've learned this and I'm going to make sure it's followed. I was really disappointed that it wasn't followed the way that it should have been. I learned all these laws saying it's a public education and whatever the child needs is what they get. "It's not the truth, it's just not the truth." I've been told he has rights to a free and appropriate education. Appropriate is the key word. It doesn't mean he gets the best of everything; just appropriate. To me, that's where the trouble is in the process. I am a proponent of the process especially now that I, Intervention Specialist, am running the IEP and ETR meetings at my school. When I started we didn't have a school psychologist, so I wrote the ETR and I contracted out with a* *psychologist. The current psychologist can't believe I did all that by myself; it blows her mind. But I am so glad I had a chance to do all the IEPs and ETRs because I understand them and now I can explain them to my families because I want them to understand it. It really is a process, a team process, and that's what makes it strong. No decision can be made by one person. You need the parent, the district rep, and the special education teacher, and the majority rules. I wouldn't want the burden of making the decision. This way, you bring in all the experts—what a solid program that is. I was really disappointed with Matthew's IEP meetings. It was very clear he needed help in everything. They were bargaining what they are going to give him help in. It was very disheartening. Our first ETR ended up in the superintendent's office because I was ready to start due process. They didn't want to give him vision services and Matthew is blind and it didn't make sense to me why they denied services. There were so many challenges that the special education supervisor talked with me and was able to get the superintendent to make some changes. I just kind of accepted where things were. They were good enough, not the best, for*

Matthew. I worked myself through weighing the process that this was good as it was going to get. I didn't have the time or money for due process. What he was getting was good and it was going to have to be good enough. Just going through this process and knowing that this meeting was so full of inconsistencies. I felt as a parent that these people just couldn't believe I was going push. They see me coming and it's like, "Oh my gosh!" I still feel this way but it doesn't bother me. This is the district I grew up, I taught in, and I supported for 42 years, but I feel like they see me and they want to run. I try to be cognizant of that and try to go in the meetings with a positive attitude, so that maybe it will be a good experience. I felt like I was causing problems and they didn't like that. That experience was very difficult. I thought it was common sense. "Why is it such a challenge?"

Couples experiences

11.11.13 (JK). *JK: I felt like they were negative with attitude when I was by myself but with my husband they were negative **without** attitude.*

2.25.13 (DG). *DG: The questions are more directed to my husband when he attends.*

What Do You Have in Your Hands Dorcus?

Summary

It was quilting time, so the teacher gave every student a piece of material to be threaded to the larger quilt. Various sorts of fabric such as black, white, striped, silk, and wool were handed—all were unique and special. One student was unhappy with the piece of material that she was given. She said, "This one is different, it doesn't look like everyone else's". The teacher replied, "Yes, your piece is different just like everyone else's, so what are you going to do with it"? The teacher began to tell the students a short biblical story of a woman named Dorcus, a well-loved seamstress who made clothes for the poor. Dorcus was a favorite of God's for she was blessed with special talents to make beautiful clothing out of some of the most tattered and unique pieces of material. The teacher asked, "What if Dorcus told God she only wanted the finest pieces of materials?" Well, one student said, "Dorcus's talents would never have been

151

appreciated." Another said, "Maybe that one piece of tattered material is the piece that helps bring everything together". So, the teacher asked, "Students, what do **you** have in **your hands?**"

Analogy

Much like Dorcus, parents of children who live with special needs are the chosen ones to cultivate and advocate for their special gifts from GOD—their children. Children's disabilities are unique and special in their own right as no two are just alike. These children may not play, walk, look, speak, grow, or behave in the same way as a typical healthy growing child. Their purpose may not be obvious to others but for their parents it is crystal clear. The true treasures of life such as blessing, supporting, loving, compassion, laughter, happiness, courage, dignity, patience and trusting are elevated to another level just because of their child's existence. And, so the question, "Parents, what do you have in your hands to make the difference from your experiences to influence special education, society, and the world and raise the level of knowledge and consciousness through your narratives?" If nothing else their stories deserve to be heard.

9.25.12 (Couple I). Husband: *We've been through so much and we want to help any parent or child get through the process. What we've gone through hasn't been for the benefit of our child but for someone else. It's parents' responsibility to raise their children, it isn't up to the school.* **Wife:** *Having a child with multiple disabilities, I don't think I would change it now but to say this when we first started. I wouldn't change him for the world. He sees the world in a completely different light than everyone else. It would be nice to see the world in a different way.* **Husband:** *Whatever he's happy with in doing in life and he's successful, not necessarily what society tells us they have to be, but what is best for them.*

4.19.13 (DW). DW: *Keep a front picture of this child's needs as it should govern everything that happens. Not, "We don't have enough money for that" or "This person doesn't have enough time." I don't want to hear that. First, it violates the law to say that. Second, it's unprofessional. You don't just put a stop sign and tell someone, "No we can't." It's important to be positive and realize the process itself. Some parents shy away with this because they don't like conflict. It* *helps support them and cope with their own emotions as they struggle both their child's needs and the difficulty of accepting the limitation of their child because the IEP at least assists in recognizing the needs.*

10.5.12 (SD). **SD:** *Schools need to start focusing more earlier on in getting these kids to ready to start trying to start to do things on self-care.*

9.24.12 (Couple 2). *Wife: They need to make the IEPs less about the paperwork. For instance, It's seems like it is more important for them to put things on his IEP because what he should be working on in his grade level but it's something they're not focused on. Husband: They need to take the chance to know the parents so they can understand the kid. Wife: You can't put everyone in the same mode. Husband: Keep the parents informed so we can work on things with our children at home. The teacher now is great—she communicates with us. Wife: She emails us twice a week; sends a communication log. Husband: We asked the year before to write and communicate with us; we even bought a journal but they wouldn't do it. Wife: If they were more specific to what the child needs and break it down. State the steps so* *we know what our kids need to reach their goals, step by step, detail by detail.*

7.11.13(JH). JH: *The IEP and the process itself should be taught to parents. I don't know what that is. Maybe because of my job as an Intervention Specialist and me working with grades nine through twelve and some seventh graders, I see these parents are coming in here and their children are in the ninth-grade and have been on an IEP for years and they have no idea. I'm thinking, I'm going to make a difference. These parents and their kids are going to understand this process. It isn't rocket science and it actually makes sense. I am floored that at this grade that parents and students are still not getting it. I have tried and they still don't understand. So, then I think maybe it's not the system. Maybe the parents have too much on them. I don't know. The students not knowing what's on their IEPs' and what accommodations are offered speaks to them not getting it. There are so many laws and regulations placed on the people writing these documents. Then, they try to stick all these rules and regulations in IEPs. That's why the public school is so "cookie cutter". They don't*

155

have time to individualize. I know it's tough because I write them.

Every time I write an IEP. I do it a little bit different. I go to an in-

service and I say, "Oh my gosh, I thought I was doing this right."

Now, they are saying you have to have this number and that number,

do this assessment before you can do this. There is just so much and to

be honest I don't think the State of Ohio understands the process so

much, much less get the people in the in-service to understand. I think

this is where the flaw is. I think we need to get a system that isn't so

hard. I love the fact that you have to back everything up, that each

section supports the other; it's a reason for each section. I don't think

it is a clear understanding about that even from the people writing it.

So, how do we get the people they are written for to understand?

Having the knowledge from the in-services and then making them

applicable. As an Intervention Specialist, sometimes I see where it

doesn't make sense. I want my students to benefit and just when you

think you get it, they change it. My school's IEP Team has an

opportunity to evaluate how we have been working the process. We've

got to look at what we have done and see how we can improve. The last meeting they talked about so much stuff that I didn't even know

what they were talking about and I've been in education since 1994.

Scary stuff, but it changes and the state is saying that a student needs

to be on an eleventh -grade level by the time they leave eleventh-

grade. I'm like, "Whoa". So my kids have to jump five grade levels

because that's what's going have to happen and that doesn't make any

sense. That's where a lot of the breakdown is. You got the system

changing and depending on who you talk to is to what that even is. It's

funny, you ask the question "How can my experience influence special

education practices and policies regarding IEPs?" I ask myself this

question all the time. I'm supposed to do something big because of

Matthew. I don't know what that is. I feel like I have to educate and

help people through the process. I've got my best understanding of the

process because I was the Special Education Department at my

school. I had to figure out and do all the aspects of everyone's job

because I was the only one. I had the practice of having to do it over

and it makes sense. I believe working with the parents as early as

possible when they are overwhelmed and just trying to accept the process. It's trying to get the word out and I'm just trying to touch

anyone who comes in my space, family or friends.

11.11.13 (JK). *JK: Stop comparing; your baby is unique. Enjoy them for who they are.*

4.19.13 (DW). *DW: "That to me was a very clear moment to me... you need to get on with it. **This is what you have...this is what you have.***"

CHAPTER 5: SUMMARY AND DISCUSSION

Introduction

The intent of this chapter is to discuss the findings and interpretations from the insights extrapolated from the stories of ten parents' experiences behind and beyond the doors of an IEP meeting. This chapter will also discuss recommendations from my knowledge gained to inform leadership in special education about parent engagement, policies and practices, as well as concluding thoughts and suggestions for future research and limitations.

Summary

The intent of this study was to listen and provide a missing voice in our understanding of the individualized education program (IEP) process through narratives of ten parents' experiences who have children on IEPs. This interpretive study was guided by the two basic assumptions that knowledge is socially constructed and researchers should attempt to comprehend the lived phenomenon from the point of view of those who lived it. This narrative inquiry not only permitted me to capture the experiences of these ten parents during their child's

IEP, but also illuminated the heartfelt power of their reflective accounts. This study also demonstrated how a researcher's transparent interestedness and multiple identities as a mother of a child who is identified under the federal disability category "multiple disabilities" with an IEP and an authority on education conveys more trustworthiness than the illusion of disinterestedness that has traditionally been practiced in qualitative inquiry. Hearing a parent's perspective of their child's IEP produces a gateway to their experience. Excluding such insight may be the awakening that increases knowledge to eradicate maladaptive practices and affirm or also develop the positive behaviors needed to afford parents a positive and productive experience in the IEP process (Garriott, Wandry & Snyder,2000).

Statement of the Problem

There is an absence of parents' voices in research on the IEP. Thus, this study intended not only to listen and provide a missing voice in our understanding of the individualized education program (IEP) through the experiences offered in the narratives of ten parents who have children on IEPs, but it also examined what those experiences tell us about how issues of power inform the process.

Purpose of the Study

The purpose of this study was to provide a parent's perspective about the IEP in order to improve this process for parents. Parents' narratives inherently have the ability to reveal the experience of their child's IEP. This will also create awareness and challenge assumptions among those stakeholders involved in the development of an IEP. This study should inform and sensitize special education professionals about parents' experiences in the IEP (Pruitt, Wandry, & Hollums, 1998). In other words, when school officials listen and understand the experiences of parents involving their children, a collaborative effort from a collective body of knowledge can decide on an individualized education plan in the best interest of that child. Thus, to bridge experiences is to build on perspectives (Garriott, P. P., Wandry, D., & Snyder, L., 2000).

Question for the Study

The research question for this study was "What do parents' narratives reveal about their experience with their child's IEP?" In answering this question, several sub-questions were also pursued including but not limited to: What do parents' narratives reveal about how power is negotiated? To what extent do parents' narratives suggest that they felt as if their voices were heard in the process? What did parents' narratives reveal about metamessages? How did parents' narratives describe their comprehension of the dialogue? To what extent do these narratives suggest that parents felt included or excluded? To what degree do parents' narratives illustrate a spirit of encouragement in the longevity of the process? And, to what extent do these narratives reveal an experience that parents felt actually worked in the best interest of their child?

FINDINGS, INTERPRETATIONS AND RECOMMENDATIONS

Alice in Wonderland

Summary

Alice in Wonderland is a classic storybook fable written by Lewis Carroll in 1865 that tells of a young girl situated in a land of mystic wonder with unfamiliar characters and dealings. She is overcome by directives and quandaries that, to say the least, are daunting. Fortunately, Alice's adventures are all but a dream as she emerges from her nap and life goes on as she knew it.

Analogy

Parents' initial experience during their child's individualized education program in special education in some cases is unfamiliar land. Like Alice, parents are confronted with directives reinforced by policies and procedures. However, these parents have a much higher stake—their child. Unlike Alice, this is the "new normal" for them. They do not wake up from a dream and live life as it was.

163

Interpretation of Narratives

According to this study's findings, most of the parents' experiences with their first IEP meetings were not positive. Those narratives that expressed positive experiences also expressed disappointment with subsequent IEP experiences. This seems to be consistent with other studies that reported on parents' first and subsequent experience with IEPs (Flanagan, 2001; Fish, 2004; Jones, 2006; Hammond, Ingalls, Trussell, 2008; Valle, 2009; Harris, 2010). School authorities need to keep in mind when collecting and reporting data and actually conducting the Evaluation Team Report (ETR) and IEP, that although this is a familiar process for them, parents may not be accustomed to the process.

Recommendations

Attitudes are informed and supported by our pre-understanding (Ryan, 2011). So, school authorities should be pro-active in ensuring a parent's understanding of the IEP process before the first meeting. Parents probably enter their first IEP meeting with a reasonable amount of anxiety, but, with an understanding of what to expect, they will have a certain amount of confidence. Hence, they can walk away with a positive attitude from their first IEP experience. Schools should not only prepare parents with literature on their rights and roles such as *"Whose IDEA is This?"* in the IEP process, but also demonstrate the difference between a positive and negative IEP. In other words, parents need to not only read about their role but also see a demonstration of the possibilities of their roles. School personnel should encourage parents to play an active role in the IEP development. In a study conducted by Jones (2006) that involved a mini-conference intervention before the actual IEP meeting to determine if parent participation would increase, it was revealed that, although there was no difference in parent participation, there was an increase in the level of satisfaction of the parents' IEP experience because of the mini-conference intervention. I recommend extending this intervention to not just a single meeting but perhaps a series of interactive experiential workshops and trainings so the information can be digested in smaller bites. It is the responsibility of the district and those in special education to support and sustain an engaged interactive program that is key to providing family-centered services. Parents should be empowered through information and education and encouraged to find their voices early in the IEP process so that the chances are increased for them to understand and embrace the concept.

The "New Normal"

Summary

This aphorism refers to the manner of which a person's usual way of knowing or dealing with a situation or life has been significantly altered. Therefore, it is a different way of doing something.

Analogy

The "new normal" to a parent raising a child who lives with special needs begins when their child is born. In some cases, the parent may not have a medical diagnosis of their child's disability. So, another dimension of "new normal" may set in when there is an acceptance of their child's condition as their lives will be affected from every domain. There will be positive and negative facets in the challenges that are surely attached to the "new normal". Every

dimension of life such as simple daily living, personal lifestyle,

relationships, finances, school, and health care will be affected.

Interpretation of Narratives

The narratives illustrated the countless ways and various

degrees of challenges within the "new normal". Most importantly, the

narratives included insight about their lives beyond the IEP meeting

and how they make meaning of their "new normal" life. It is an epic

lifestyle alteration from simple daily home tasks to having an

enjoyable outing in their community. Indisputably, life beyond special

education, such as personal lives were changed in a multitude of ways

as well. According to these findings, parents' lives are dictated by

daily challenges consisting of stressful decisions and strenuous

schedules for their children in some of the following ways: preparing

for a school day or regular day, feeding and dressing them,

administering medications, dealing with incontinence, doctor and

hospital visits, and therapy. There are countless dealings with various

agencies, entities, and individuals to support the well-being of their

167

child such as insurance companies, home health care businesses, independent providers, specialists, and the school system. It appears that the more complex the child's diagnosis or condition is, the more stress, the more entities, and individuals are in their lives. At times, this must be scary because people are constantly coming in and out their homes and lives. In addition, there are physical, mental, and health encounters for the parents themselves. As one parent pointed out, she cannot afford the time to have surgery on a torn muscle as a result of maneuvering her son from one position to another. Another parent shared how the growth of her son has become a threat to her and her son's teachers. Exhausting hospital admissions not only takes a toll on the child but also on the parents. Mental stress is just as damaging, especially if the child has a life threatening diagnosis as some of these parents shared. Challenges are pressed upon them in numerous ways and some challenges may be untimely.

Recommendations

The implication for education authorities in special education is to know the families you are servicing. If you know your families, you are empathetic to their needs. Thus, you can better serve them. Taking the time to build relationships with the families is imperative to sustaining trust and value. Teachers should embrace the concept "funds of knowledge" (Moll, Amanti, Neff, and Gonzalez, 2001) as it allows the teachers to have a better understanding; thus, a connection to the child and their families. Funds of knowledge are capable of truly designing an IEP for that student culturally and cognitively. This new found knowledge of the family's life beyond special education allows the team to understand how the child functions in their household and as an individual. This is an invaluable resource that can only be conveyed from the child and their family.

The Gingerbread Boy

Summary

This classic tale from the May 1875, issue of *St. Nicholas Magazine* is about an elderly couple that longed for additional company. So, the elderly lady bakes a gingerbread boy who sprang from the oven and outruns both she and her husband. He continues to outrun everyone who sets out to catch him. Unfortunately, he finds his match with a sly fox and the gingerbread boy succumbs to his demise.

Analogy

Parents' having concerns of the individualized education program (IEP) being less than what the name implies was frequently voiced. In some narratives, the term "cookie cutter" was used. The comparison between The Gingerbread Boy and an IEP is not in the plot of the story but in the details that create each outcome. Hence, the irony is in the systemic manufacturing of each product. For instance, the traditional gingerbread boy cookie components are the eyes, mouth, arms, legs, and buttons for clothing. In comparison, the IEP components are the present levels of academic performance, annual goals; benchmarks or short-term goals, measuring and reporting progress, special education and related services, supplementary aids, and program modifications or individual accommodations. Depending on the age and grade of the student, the IEP may contain additional content. The details of the creation of the gingerbread boy and an IEP are essential in the function of each product. However, the lack of individuality for a gingerbread cookie is much more acceptable than the lack of it in an IEP. From a parents' perspective, individuality is what is significant in the value for their child's success. Hence, the "cookie cutter" model should not be valid in the IEP process.

Interpretation of Narratives

Twenty-five percent of the parents from this study used the term "cookie cutter" to describe their child's IEP. Another 37.5% shared how individuality is imperative to understanding children living with special needs. The parents from this study have a good sense of what individuality means in terms of their children being academically successful.

Recommendations

Individualizing an IEP is contingent upon how well you know the student on a personal level. Educational authorities must allow themselves to be learners and listeners of the families, so they can understand and cultivate skills they may not have known their students possess. Funds of knowledge will allow this, it takes time and resources to put forth this effort, but the increase of success for the

171

student is well worth the time. Having the teacher visit the child's home would be very helpful in retrieving funds of knowledge. In addition, the school might develop social events or a movie video showcasing the child and the family to achieve a great portion of this knowledge. Parents and school staff will need to collaborate on achievable means to learn more about the child. Lack of resources and time should not be a road block in trying to retrieve pertinent information such as funds of knowledge.

Groundhog Day

Summary

Groundhog Day is a 1993, American comedy starring Bill Murray who plays an arrogant and narcissistic television weatherman who is forced to re-evaluate his life and ethical center after covering a Groundhog Day event. He continues to relive the same detailed actions every morning he awakens. What's further disturbing and perplexing is that those around him appear to be moving about their day in a mechanical and mundane manner. He seems to be trapped in a never ending timeless loop.

Analogy

Groundhog Day was the way a parent in my interview piloting process expressed her frustration with the IEP. I thought it was a brilliant expression in how she made meaning of the sometimes repetitive mechanical actions of the staff and special education system

Interpretation of Narratives

According to this research, some parents felt that school professionals perform in a mechanical manner when it came to their child's IEP. In other words, school professionals are more interested or trained in the status quo rather than the individual student. This led the parents to describe the goals applied to IEPs as for the sake of academic standards and not their child's ability. These parents' narratives expressed that the repetitive nature of IEP meetings were frustrating. This may leave families to believe that the schools are not valuing time or the best interest of their child. Apparently, the IEP documents are being viewed only during the time of the IEP meeting and not looked at again until the next meeting. It is possible that these students are not being monitored and documentation of their activities is not being taken. If it weren't so, "Groundhog Day" episodes would not occur. Otherwise, if there were no gains from previously set goals, then adjustments should be made. If the IEP is treated as a living and breathing document, it will always be current because the teacher is monitoring, documenting, and addressing the child's needs for progression.

Aha Moment

Summary

An "aha moment" is an aphorism that refers to the enlightenment, realization, and understanding of something. It is an awakening of a consciousness during a meaningful situation.

Analogy

The journey of living a life as a parent of a child living with special needs is a continuous learning trajectory. In some cases the "aha moment" begins in the acceptance of their "new normal".

Interpretation of Narratives

The lessons learned for the parent participants in this study came to them in many different ways, but the common thread of becoming better advocates for their children was paramount. There is no one way to do this as explained in various stories. What works for some parents may not be suitable or natural to others. For instance, I thought it was interesting that JK described one of her lessons learned was of allowing the school authorities to speak since the parent should remain quiet and listen because school officials know more about what to do with the child. A parent's role in the IEP team process is of equal value. The Individual with Disabilities Education Act (IDEA '97) further expanded parents' rights to participate in the decision making process. Perhaps JK's response may have been as a result of a lack of

understanding that it is a parents' right to be an equal decision- making participant. This further questions if this sort of information is being shared and not just through the booklet *Whose IDEA is This? A Parent's Guide to the Individuals with Disability Education Improvement Act 2004(IDEA)*. According to this study, only 25% of the parents saw any true purpose in the book. Others thought the book was not parent-friendly or too confusing. It is worth mentioning that the 25% of parents who actually read and saw a purpose for the book were educators.

Accountability, Power and Rights ...Oh My!

Summary

This aphorism was taken from the classical chant in "The Wizard of Oz" when Dorothy, Scarecrow, and Tinman were walking through the frightening forest—"Lions and Tigers and Bears...Oh My!" Naturally, they were fearful of the unknown—of the possibilities within the wicked forest.

Analogy

The likeness of this to the IEP process is in the unspoken, imagined fear behind the words accountability, power, and rights. The phrase "Oh my" tends to heighten the possibilities. All three words can be imagined in the lives of parents introduced to special education. There are parents who never had to deal with these terms from an academic perspective until they entered the forest of Special Education. The efficacy of these words will be realized from the parents' narrative response.

Interpretation of Narratives

In this study, parents declared their agency. For some, it took several encounters. For others it was inherent due to their teaching backgrounds and prior observations. Power asymmetries resonated throughout their stories. According to these parents' experiences, one hears power negotiated through developing the IEP document, metamessages exhibited in the IEP meetings, overt dialogue, and behaviors exhibited by school authorities. In addition, it was apparent that as a parent of a child on IEP, one has to know when to compromise and when to advocate. It's unfortunate that parents felt that the concept of an IEP team meeting is reduced, in some cases, to a bargaining table. This cannot simply be because their child is involved. I suspect every caring parent would first choose **the best** for their child not **second best** or what the law says is **"appropriate"**. However, I suppose in having to choose between

nothing or **appropriate**, the latter prevails. Parent participant **7.11.13(JH)** painted the following illustration in her story that better explains "nothing" and "appropriate". *"I just kind of accepted where things were. They were good enough, not the best, for Matthew. I worked myself through weighing the process that this was good as it was going to get. I didn't have the time or money for due process. What he was getting was good and it was going to have to be good enough."* What I conclude from this parent's excerpt was "appropriate" is, not the best, good—it is adequate. This was not an easy decision as I connected with her emotional resonance. This was one example, of many, where the parent participant's emotional tones were not apparent through the text. Due process protects the rights of parents and their children who live with disabilities. A hearing can take place at the request of the parent or agency to resolve a due process complaint (ODE, 2012). The due process hearing can be timely and expensive.

Recommendations

Parent participant's, 7.11.13(JH), excerpt is apropos to the following recommendation. Be advised not to be trusting to low due process status (Doug Goldberg, 2012). Just because your school has not experienced due process, does not mean that parents are satisfied with the IEP. Attrition rates in parent satisfaction may be on an incline. Special education authorities should answer the following questions: "How do you want parents to experience their IEP process?"; "How do you measure parents' experiences with their IEP process?", and "What mechanisms do you have in place to address parents' needs?" No data is worth having without being undergirded

with truth from participants. It is the schools responsibility to make sure parents feel comfortable and safe to voice their concerns (B. Flanagan, 2001).

What do You Have in Your Hands Dorcus?

Summary

It was quilting time, so the teacher gave every student a piece of material to be threaded to the larger quilt. Various sorts of fabric

179

such as black, white, striped, silk, and wool were handed—all were unique and special. One student was unhappy with the piece of material that she was given. She said, "This one is different, it doesn't look like everyone else's". The teacher replied, "Yes, your piece is different just like everyone else's, so what are you going to do with it"? The teacher began to tell the students a short biblical story of a woman named Dorcus, a well-loved seamstress who made clothes for the poor. Dorcus was a favorite of God's for she was blessed with special talents to make beautiful clothing out of some of the most tattered and unique pieces of material. The teacher asked, "What if Dorcus told God she only wanted the finest pieces of materials?" Well, one student said, "Dorcus's talents would never have been appreciated." Another said, "Maybe that one piece of tattered material is the piece that helps bring everything together". So, the teacher asked, "Students, what do **you** have in **your hands?**"

Analogy

Much like Dorcus, parents of children who live with special needs are the chosen ones to cultivate and advocate for their special gifts from GOD—their children. Children's disabilities are unique and special in their own right as no two are just alike. These children may not play, walk, look, speak, grow, or behave in the same way as a typical healthy growing child. Their purpose may not be obvious to others but for their parents it is crystal clear. The true treasures of life such as blessing, loving, compassion, laughter, happiness, courage, dignity, patience and trusting are elevated to another level just because of their child's existence. And, so the question, "Parents, what do you have in your hands to make the difference from your experiences to

influence special education, society, and the world and raise the level of knowledge and consciousness through your narratives?" If nothing else their stories deserve to be heard.

Interpretation of Narratives

The parents in this study not only know what makes their children successful in their everyday life but also what would make for developing a successful IEP for parents in the future or at the least for their children. They seem to understand what they have in their hands (their experiences) to make a difference in special education, society, and the world. They understood their child's individuality. They knew

that other members of the team provide crucial information, ideas, and

the benefits of their knowledge and experience. Most importantly, they

understand that their child is the center and the team should surround

support around their child. They comprehend that they too have a

voice for information, ideas, knowledge, and experience; their voices

are just as important, if not more important, than any other member. I

detected a

common whisper of developing an IEP that is potential-centered. For

anecdotal examples, I recall **10.08.12 AP's** story about how her son,

JC , was a master at the game Wheel A Fortune and **04.19.13 DW's**

story of how she had every staff member at the beginning of the IEP

meeting start off saying something positive about her son before

officially starting the meeting and the staff appreciated that beginning.

Recommendations

Special education needs to practice being potential-centered vs.

label or diagnosis-centered for their children. Potential-centered is

keeping the focus on what the child is already successfully

demonstrating at home or school and less focused on the child's label or diagnosis and what research or texts say their child can and cannot do. This is not to say there is no place for diagnosis, but it should only serve as a backdrop and for medical intervention. We can get caught up with labels and categories which blur our vision of the child's potential.

One of the several poignant concerns from this study that struck me was **04.19.13 DW's** cry for someone who carries out the coordination of the implementation of the IEP. In other words, what I understood her to say is that the oversights that take place are not monitored and when she requests to get information she is shut out or given the run around. It's like she felt she was in this program alone until she makes cacophonic sounds and demonstrates resistance when only is she heard. This must be a lonely feeling. Special education must do a better job in sensitizing the coordination of continuity and integration of the IEP. I recommend practicing attunement. A clinical definition of attunement is a level of connection that leads both the patient and clinician to resonate to be on one accord—in harmony (Koloroutis and

Trout, 2012). In order for attunement to take place, the clinician must be emotionally willing and authentically attentive to the patient as a human being (Koloroutis and Trout, 2012).

CONCLUDING THOUGHTS

The parent participants in this study were loving parents and passionate advocates for their children. These parents exemplified the definition of experts in the knowledge of their children's academic and personal successes. Their knowledge would serve nothing less than rich and resourceful information within the individualized education program.

Special education, what do you have in your hands? Speaking as an authority in education, I believe educators' and school administrators' intentions are in the best interest of students. Unfortunately, intentions will not galvanize the school, especially special education, system to move in a transformative era, if we are not in attunement. I strongly believe that the medical and education models are inextricably aligned. Again, an aspect of my purpose for conducting such a study was to sensitize the coordination of continuity and integration of the IEP development.

Several parent participants' narratives echoed my personal narrative as a mother and as an authority in education. I believe this revelation supports my claim that my transparent interestedness and subjectivities as a researcher conveys more trustworthiness than the illusion of disinterestedness that has traditionally been practiced in qualitative inquiry. It was emancipating to hear like narratives that made me want to respond, "That's my story." I never met some of these parent participants before the interview. Most interestingly and validating, none of these parents had ever heard my story. Nonetheless, the emotional power of the stories that were told and supported by the deep meanings of our experiences united us.

I am a scholar and researcher who believes that exposing one's subjectiveness should not brand the work as being any less scholarly, politically engaging, skewed or biased. Indeed, it is the epitome of transparency and places the work at the forefront of being challenged. There is nothing problematic about being transparent in one's subjectiveness. However, one should engage in being introspective—reflexive in their work. Individuals expressing an opposing perspective should be welcomed as it advances the discourse and furthers research. However, there is much to say about someone who posits themselves as being value-free (Greenbank, 2003).

Limitations

While efforts were made to try to convey the emotional power of the parents' stories, there is no comparison to actually hearing their voice inflections when describing their experiences. There were actually 16 parent participants who agreed and scheduled to be interviewed. However, eight participants did not follow through with explanation. Unfortunately, one narrative was mistakenly erased while getting acclimated to new recording technology. While efforts were made to have a diverse group of parent participants, there was only one narrative from a parent whose child was a female. Therefore, an argument as to whether or not the gender of a child has an impact on a parent's IEP experience has yet to be researched.

Suggestions for Future Research

A future study might include the narratives of stakeholders such as regular and special education teachers, psychologist, or other school representatives. While this study recruited those parents whose children were identified under the federal disability category "multiple disabilities" and "developmental delays" grades one through eight, perhaps a study that focuses on an isolated disability might suggest different results. Whether gender impacts a parents' experience within the IEP is another possible area for future research.

Appendix A

Where Are the Parents?
By Sue Stuyvesant, Parent

Hey everyone. For those of you who don't know me (I'm only an occasional poster) I am mom to Michelle, 9 years old, microcephalic, athetoid/spastic CP, cortical visual impairment, seizure disorder -- and CUTE! OK, now for the reason I'm posting.

To make a long story short, earlier this week a question was asked by some nitwit official as to why there weren't more parents (of special needs kids) involved in the local PTA and other issues that have come up that directly involve our kids. His question, which was passed on to me was, "Where are the parents?" I went home that night, started thinking - and boy was I pi**ed - and banged this "little" essay out the next day on my lunch break. By the way, I took copies of this to the school board meeting that night, gave it to a couple of influential people and it WILL get around......

Where are the parents?

They are on the phone to doctors and hospitals and fighting with insurance companies, wading through the red tape in order that their child's medical needs can be properly addressed. They are buried under a mountain of paperwork and medical bills, trying to make sense of a system that seems designed to confuse and intimidate all but the very savvy.

Where are the parents?

They are at home, diapering their 15 year old son, or trying to lift their 100 lb. daughter onto the toilet. They are spending an hour at each meal
to feed a child who cannot chew, or laboriously and carefully feeding

their child through a g-tube. They are administering medications, changing catheters and switching oxygen tanks.

Where are the parents?

They are sitting, bleary eyed and exhausted, in hospital emergency rooms, waiting for tests results to come back and wondering, "Is this the time when my child doesn't pull through?" They are sitting patiently in hospital rooms as their child recovers from yet another surgery to lengthen hamstrings or straighten backs or repair a faulty internal organ. They are waiting in long lines in county clinics because no insurance company will touch their child.

Where are the parents?

They are sleeping in shifts because their child won't sleep more than 2 or 3 hours a night, and must constantly be watched, lest he do himself, or another member of the family, harm. They are sitting at home with their child because family and friends are either too intimidated or too unwilling to help with child care and the state agencies that are designed to help are suffering cut backs of their own.

Where are the parents?

They are trying to spend time with their non-disabled children, as they try to make up for the extra time and effort that is critical to keeping their disabled child alive. They are struggling to keep a marriage together, because adversity does not always bring you closer. They are working 2 and sometime 3 jobs in order to keep up with the extra expenses. And sometimes they are a single parent struggling to do it all by themselves.

Where are the parents?

They are trying to survive in a society that pays lip service to helping those in need, as long as it doesn't cost them anything. They are trying to patch their broken dreams together so that they might have some sort of normal life for their children and their families.

They are busy, trying to survive!

Sue Stuyvesant 10/15/96: Permission to duplicate or distribute this document is granted with the provision that the document remains intact.

Sue passed away in October 2003. Michelle passed away a week before she was to turn 18 in September 2005.

References

Argus-calvo, B., Tafoya, N. G., & Grupp, L. L. (2005). Pre referral: A
time to empower culturally and linguistically diverse families
through a family-centered approach. . . *Multiple Voices, 8(1),*
71-83.

Atkinson, P., & Silverman, D. (1997). Kundera's immortality: The
interview society and the invention of the self. *Qualitative
Inquiry, 3,* 304-325.

Banks, & Banks (2005). (Ed.). : . []. http://dx.doi.org/. Retrieved from

Banks, S. A. (1982). Once upon a time: Interpretation in literature and
medicine. *Literature and Medicine, 1,* 23-27. Retrieved from

Bessell, A. (2001, September). Educating children with chronic illness.
Exceptional Parent Maagazine, 44-48.

Bigner, J. J. (2013). Parenting special needs children. Retrieved from
http://www.education.com/print/parenting-children-special-
needs/

Bochner, A. (2001). . *Narrative's virtues, 7 (2),* 131-157.

Bold, C. (2012). *Using narrative in research*. Thousand Oaks, CA:

    SAGE.

Brueggemann, B. J. (1999). *Lend me your ear*. Washington, DC:

    Gallauder University Press.

Bruner, J. (2002). *Making stories: Law, literature, life*. Cambridge,

    MA: Harvard University Press.

Butler-Kisber, L. (2010). *Qualitative inquiry*. London: SAGE.

Caines, B. (1998). Views from the other side: Parental perceptions of

    the individualized educational plan IEP process (Masters

    Thesis). Available from National Library of Canada. (0-612-

    33814-2)

Categories of disabilities under IDEA. (2010). Retrieved from

    http://nichcy.org

Childre, A., & Chambers, C. (, September 2005). Family perceptions

    of student centered planning and IEP meetings. *Education and

    Training in Developmental Disabilities, 40 n3*, 217-233.

Clancy, M. (2013). Is reflexivity the key to minimizing problems of

interpretation in phenomenological research? *Nurse*

Researcher, 20, 12-16. Retrieved from

Clandinin, D. J., & Connelly, F. M. (2000). *Narrative inquiry:*

Experience and story in qualitative research. San Fransisco,

CA: Jossey-Bass.

Clandinin, D. J., Puchor, D., & Murry Orr, A. (2007). Navigating sites

for narrative inquiry. *Journal of Teacher Education, 58:21.*

http://dx.doi.org/10.1177/0022487106296218

Clandinin, D. J., Pushor, D., & Orr, A. M. (2007, January/February).

Navigating sites for narrative inquiry. *Journal of Teacher*

Education, 58 No. 1, 21-35. Retrieved from sagepub.com

Cottie, M. (2012, May 7). When love is not enough. *Newsweek, 159*

issue 19, 38-42.

Creswell, J. W. (1998). Qualitative inquiry and research design:

Choosing among five traditions (1st Ed.). California: Sage.

Dabkowski, D. M. (2004). Encouraging active parent participation in

    IEP team meetings. *Teaching Exceptional Children, Vol. 36,*

    No. 33, 34-39.

Denzin, N. K., & Lincoln, Y. S. (1994). Introduction: Entering the

    field of qualitative research. In handbook of qualitative

    research. Thousand Oak, CA: Sage.

Diament, M. (2012, January 24). Most parents pleased with IEP.

    Special Education Advisor. http://dx.doi.org/14844

Duttenhoffer, J. (2010). Factors influencing the spectrum of emotions

    parents experience. Retrieved from

    http://www.examiner.com/special-education-in-

    baltimore/janelle-duttenhoffer?page=1

Elliot, J. (2005). *Using narrative in social research.* : London: Sage

    Publications.

Fish, W. W. (2008). The IEP meeting: Perception of parents of

    students who receive special education services. *Preventing*

    School Failure, 53 n 1, 8-14.

Flanagan, B. G. (2001). *Parents' views of and participation in the special education process* (Unpublished doctoral dissertation). Virginia Polytechnic Institute and State University, Blacksburg, VI. Retrieved from

Flanigan, C. (2007). Preparing pre-service teachers to partner with parents and communities. *The School Community Journal, Vol. 17. No. 2.*

Gallagher, G., & Konjoian, P. (2010). Shut up about your perfect kid: A survival guide for ordinary parents of special chidren. : New York: Three Rivers Press.

Garriott, P. P., Synder, L., & Wandry, D. (2000). Teachers as parents, parents as children: What's wrong with this picture? *Preventing School Failures, 45,* 37-43.

Gilgun, J. F. (2008). Lived experience, reflexivity, and research on perpetrators of interpersonal violence. *Qualitative Social Work, 7 No. 2,* 181-197. http://dx.doi.org/10.1177/1473325008089629

Gilliam, J. E., & Coleman, M. C. (1981). Who influences IEP

    committee decisions? *Exceptional Children, 47,* 642-644.

Goldstein, S., Strickland, B., Turnbull, A., & Curry, L. (1980). An

    observational analysis of the IEP conference. *Exceptional*

    Children, Vol. 46, No. 4, 278-286.

Greenbank, P. (2013, January 2). The role of values in educational

    research: the case for reflexivity. *British Educational Research*

    Journal, 29 Iss 6, 791–801.

Guba, E., & Lincoln, Y. S. (1994). *Do inquiry paradigms imply*

    inquiry methodologies? Thousands Oak, CA: Sage.

Hammond, H., Ingalls, L., & Trussell, R. P. (2008). Family members'

    involvement in the initial individual education program (IEP)

    meeting and the IEP process: Perceptions and reactions.

    International Journal about Parents in Education, 2 No. 1, 35-

    48. Retrieved from

    www.ernape.net/ejournal/index.php/IJPE/article/download/70/

    55

Harris, A. (2010). Parental and professional participation in the IEP process: A comparison of Discourses (Doctoral dissertation). Available from ProQuest LLC.

Harry, B. (1992). Cultural diversity, families, and the special education system: Communication and empowerment. : New York: Teachers College Press.

Harry, B. (2008, March 22). Collaboration with culturally and linguistically diverse families: ideal versus reality. *Exceptional Children*.

Heifetz, R. (1994). *Leadership without easy answers*. United States of America: Library of Congress Cataloging.

Hildebrand, V. P., Phenice, L. A., Gray, M. M., & Hines, R. P. (2000). *Knowing and serving diverse families* (2nd Ed.). : Pearson.

Hiles, D. R. (2008). Transparency. In Butler-Kisber, Lynn (2010). Qualitative inquiry. London: SAGE.

Huefner, D. S. (2000). The risks and opportunities of the IEP requirements under IDEA '97. *The Journal of Special Education, 33, 195-204.*

IDEA: Individuals with Disabilities Education Improvement Act, 34
Code of Federal Regulations § 300.321 (2004).

Islam, Z., Farjana, S., & Shanaz, R. (2013, January 1). Stress among
parents of children with mental retardation. *Bangladesh
Journal of Medical Science, 12 No. 12*, 74-80.

Janus, M., Kopechanski, L., Cameron, R., & Hughes, D. (2008). .
Early Childhood Education Journal, 35 (5), 479-485.

Johnson, J., & Duffett, A. (2002). When it's your own child: Views
from parents about special education. Advance online
publication. http://dx.doi.org/

Jones, B. A. (2006). *The effects of mini-conferencing prior to IEP
meetings on parental involvement in the IEP process* (Doctoral
dissertation). Retrieved from etd.lsu.edu/docs/available/etd-
07062006-134722/unrestricted/Jones

Jootun, D. (2009, June 11). Reflexivity: Promoting rigor in qualitative
research. *Nursing Standard, 23 n23*, 23, 42-46.

Koloroutis, M., & Trout, M. (2012). *See me as a person: Creating therapeutic relationships with patients and their families.* United States of America: Creative Health Care Management.

Kroth, R. L., & Edge, D. (1997). . In Strategies for communications with parents and families of exceptional children (3rd Ed.). Denver, CO: Love.

Ladson-Billings, G. (1994). *The dreamkeepers.* San Francisco, CA: Jossey-Bass.

Lamorey, S. (2002, May-Jun 2002). The effects of culture on special education services: Evil eyes, prayer meetings, and IEPs. *TEACHING Exceptional Children, v34 n5,* p67-71 . http://dx.doi.org/Retrieved from

Latham, S. L. (2002). *Parents' perceptions of communication practices with school professionals during initial years of special education placement* (Unpublished doctoral dissertation). . Retrieved from dc.etsu.edu/cgi/viewcontent.cgi?article=1804&context=etd

Lauer (2011,). . . , (), . http://dx.doi.org/Retrieved from

Lawrence-Lightfoot, S. (2003). *Essential conversations: What parents and teachers can learn from each other*. United States of America: The Random House.

Leininger, M. (1985). Ethnography and ethno nursing: Models and modes of qualitative data analysis. *Qualitative Research Methods in Nursing*.

Lin, M. (2012). Seven things you don't' know about a special needs parent. Retrieved from http://www.huffingtonpost.com/maria-lin/special-needs-parenting_b_1314348.html

Lusthaus, C. S., Lusthaus, E. W., & Gibbs, H. (1981). Parents' role in the decision process. *Exceptional Children, Vol. 48, No.3*, 256-257.

Lynch, E., & Stein, R. (1987). Parent participation by ethnicity: A comparison of hispanic, black, and anglo families. *The Council of Exceptional Children, 54 No. 2*, 105-111.

Lytle, R. K., & Bordin, J. (2001). Enhancing the IEP team: Strategies for parents and professionals. *TEACHING Exceptional Children, Vol, 33, No. 5*, 40-44.

Martin, J., Marshall, L., & Sale, P. (2004). A three year study of middle, junior high and high school IEP meetings. *Exceptional Children, 70 No. 3*. Retrieved from http://www.questia.com/read/1G1-114328007/a-3-year-study-of-middle-junior-high-and-high-school

Mason, J. (1994). Researching from the inside in mathematical education: Locating an I-you relationship. *Centre for Mathematics Education*.

Massimilla, E. (Ed.). (1981). Heaven's very special child. Retrieved from http://specialmompreneurs.com/blog/poem-heavens-very-special-child. Verbal consent given on 7/11/16.

McKee, S. (2004, Summer/Fall). Putting perspective into the IEP: A parent-turned-professionals's view. *The National Fragile X Foundation Quarterly*, 39-40.

Mcmillan, J., & Wergin, J. (2010). *Understanding and evaluating educational research* (4 ed.). : Pearson.

Medically fragile. (2010). In. Retrieved from http://medicallyfragilechild.com/medically-fragile-dhild-definition

Mencap. (2001). No ordinary life: the support needs of families caring for children and adults with profound and multiple learning disabilities. Retrieved from http://www.mencap.org.uk/search/apachesolr_search/no%20or dinary%20life

Moore, E. (2010). Parenting a special needs child as a working mom: Balancing work and family. Retrieved from http://www.babble.com/mom/parenting-special-needs-child-balancing-work-family/

Moustakas, C. (1994). Phenomenological research methods. *Exceptional Children, 48 No.3*, 256-257.

National Council of Disability. (1995). improving implementation of the individuals with disabilities in education act: Making schools work for all of America's children. Retrieved from

http://www.ncb.gov

Ohio Department of Education (2012). Whose IDEA is this? A

parent's guide to the individuals with disabilities education

improvement act of 2004 (Ed.). Ohio: ODE.

O'donovan, E. (2007, July). Making individualized education

programs manageable for parents. , 69. Retrieved from

www.DistrictAdministration.com

Parent participation 300.322. (2007). Retrieved May 20, 2013, from

http://Ed.gov

Peshkin, A. (1988, October). In search of subjectivity--One's own.

Educational Researcher, 17-22.

Philippa, R. (2008). Building brighter futures for all our children- a

new focus on families as partners and change agents in the care

and development of children with disabilities or special

educational needs. *Support for Learning, 23 No. 3*, 106-112.

Plum, C. (2008). *Interaction within individualized education program meetings: Conversation analysis of a collective case study* (Doctoral dissertation). Retrieved from http://gradworks.umi.com/cgi-bin/redirect?url=http://gateway.proquest.com/openurl%3furl_v er=Z39.88-2004%26res_dat=xri:pqdiss%26rft_val_fmt=info:ofi/fmt:kev: mtx:dissertation%26rft_dat=xri:pqdiss:3342449

Polkinghorne, D. (1988). *Narrative knowing and the human sciences.* Albany, NY: State University of New York Press.

Pruitt, P., Wandry, D., & Hollums, D. (1998). Listen to us! Parents speak out about their interaction with special educators. *Preventing School Failure, 42(4)*, 161-166.

Reinman, J. W., Beck, L., Coppola, T., & Engiles, A. (2010). Parents' experiences with the IEP process: Considerations for improving practice. Retrieved from http://www.directionservice.org/cadre/

Richardson, L. (1990, April 1). Narrative and sociology. *Journal of Contemporary Ethnography, 19 No. 1*, 116.

Rock, M. L. (2000). Parents as equal partners: Balancing the scales in IEP development. *TEACHING Exceptional Children, Vol. 32, No. 6*, 30-37.

Ryan, T. (2011). . The New Zealand Journal of Teacher's Work, 8 (2), 220-228.

Sandelowski, M. (1991, fall 1991). Telling stories: Narrative approaches in qualitative research. *IMAGE: Journal of Nursing Scholarship, Vol. 23*, 161-166.

Schultz, S. (2011). Parenting children with special needs. Retrieved from http://www.parentmap.com/article/parenting-children-with-special-needs

Schutz, S. (1994). Exploring the benefits of a subjective approach in qualitative nursing research. *Journal of Advanced Nursing, 20*, 412-417.

Seidman, E. (2013). How special needs parenting compares to typical parenting. Retrieved from http://www.parents.com/blogs/to-the-max/2013/03/19/autism/how-special-needs-parenting-compares-to-typical-parenting/

Sheehey, P. H. (2006, fall). Parent involvement in educational decision-making: A Hawaiian perspective. *Rural special education quarterly, 25 Iss.. 4*, 3-15. Retrieved from http://www.questia.com/library/journal/1P3-1333787371/parent-involvement-in-educational-decision-making

Simon, J. B. (2006). Perceptions of the IEP requirement. *Teacher Education and Special Educaton, Vol. 29, No. 4*, 17-27.

Smith, S. (2006, May 3). Encouraging the use of reflexivity in the writing up of qualitative research. *International Journal of Therapy and Rehabilitation, 13 Iss. 5*, 209-215.

Spann, S. J., Kohler, F. W., & Soenksen, D. (2003). Examining parents' involvement in and perceptions of special education services: an interview with families in a parent support group.

Focus on Autism and Other Developmental Disabilities, Vol. 18. No. 4, 228-237.

Speziale, H., & Carpenter, D. (2007). *Qualitative research in nursing: Advancing the humanistic imperative* (4th Ed.). : Philadelphia: Lippin Cott Williams and Williams.

Staples, K. E., & Diliberto, J. A. (2010, July/Aug). Guidelines for successful parent involvement: Working with parents of students with disabilities. *Teaching Exceptional Children, 42 No. 5*, 58-63.

Stephens, S. W. (2001). *Involving parents in the IEP process* (ED455658). Retrieved from ERIC Clearinghouse on Disabilities and Gifted Education: http://www.ericdigests.org/2002-2/iep.htm

Stoner, J. B., Bock, S. J., Thompson, J. R., Angell, M. E., Heyl, B. S., & Crowley, E. P. (2005). Welcome to our world: Parents perceptions of interactions between parents of young children with ASD and education professionals. *Focus on Autism and Other Developmental Disabilities, 20 (1)*, 39-51.

Stuyvesant, S. (1996). Where Are the Parents? Retrieved from

www.frcnca.org/wp-

content/uploads/2011/08/wherearetheparnets1.doc

Tadema, A. C., & Vlaskamp, C. (2009). The time and effort in taking

care for children with profound intellectual and multiple

disabilities: A study on care load and support. *British Journal*

of Learning Disabilities, 38, 41-48.

http://dx.doi.org/10.1111/j.1468-3156.2009.00561

Transparent (n.d.). Collins English Dictionary- Complete and

Unabridged 10th Edition. Retrieved from

http://dictionary.reference.com/browse/transparent

Turnball, A., & Leonard, J. (1981). Parent involvement in special

education: Emerging advocacy roles. *School Psychology*

Review, Vol.10, No.1, 37-44.

Turnball, A., & Turnball, A. (2001). *Families, professionals and*

exceptionality: Collaborating for empowerment (4th Ed.).

Retrieved from Upper River, NJ

Turnbull, A. P., & Turnbull, H. R. (1997). *Families, professionals and exceptionality: A special partnership*. Upper Saddle River, NJ: Prentice-Hall.

Unknown author (n.d.). *Dorcus the Lord's Beloved Seamstress: Adapted version*. Retrieved from http://childrenschapel.org/biblestories/dorcas.html

Valle, J. (2009). What mothers say about special education: From the 1960's to the present. New York, NY: PALGRAVE MACMILLAN.

Valle, J. W. (2011). Down the rabbit hole: A commentary about research on parents and special education. *Learning Disability Quarterly, 34(3)*, 183-190. http://dx.doi.org/10.1177/0731948711417555

Webster, L., & Mertova, P. (2007). *Using narrative inquiry as a research method*. Milton Park, Abingdon, Oxon and New York, NY: Routledge.

Whitebread, G., Bruder, M., Fleming, G., & Park, H. (2007).

Collaboration in special education. . *Teaching Exceptional*

Children, 39(4), 6-14.

Williamson, P. A. (2011). Special needs children: A new way of life

for the family. Retrieved from

http://ezinearticles.com/?Special-Needs-Children:-A-New-

Way-of-Life-for-the-Family&id=5983373

Winters, W. (1993). African American mothers and urban schools:

The power of participation. Retrieved from

Witt, J., Miller, G. D., McIntyre, R. M., & Smith, D. (1984). Effects of

variables on parental perceptions of staffing. *The Council for*

Exceptional Children, 91 No. 1, 27-32.

Wright, P., & Wright, P. (2007). *Special education law* (2nd Ed.).

Hartfield, VA: Habor House Law Press.

Wubbels, Levy, & Brekelmans (1997,). Journal languages and

cultural factors in students' perception of teacher

communication style. *International Journal of Intercultural*

Relations.

Yoshida, R. K., & Gottlieb, J. (1977). A model of parental

participation in the pupil planning process. *Mental Retardation,

Vol. 15*, 17-20.

Printed in the United States
By Bookmasters